RECOVERING PROSPERITY THROUGH QUALITY

Also available from Quality Press

Government Quality and Productivity: Success Stories
Henry L. Lefevre, editor

Incredibly American: Releasing the Heart of Quality
Marilyn R. Zuckerman and Lewis J. Hatala

A Quality System for Education
Stanley J. Spanbauer

ASQC Total Quality Management Series
Richard S. Johnson

Principles and Practices of TQM
Thomas J. Cartin

*Benchmarking: The Search for Industry Best Practices
that Lead to Superior Performance*
Robert C. Camp

The Whats, Whys, and Hows of Quality Improvement
George L. Miller and LaRue L. Krumm

Root Cause Analysis: A Tool for Total Quality Management
Paul F. Wilson, Larry D. Dell, and Gaylord F. Anderson

To receive a complimentary catalog of publications,
call 800-248-1946.

RECOVERING PROSPERITY THROUGH QUALITY

The Midland City Story

Robert A. Schwarz

ASQC Quality Press
Milwaukee, Wisconsin

RECOVERING PROSPERITY THROUGH QUALITY:
THE MIDLAND CITY STORY
Robert A. Schwarz

Library of Congress Cataloging-in-Publication Data
Schwarz, Robert A.
  [Midland City]
  Recovering prosperity through quality: the Midland City story/
Robert A. Schwarz.
     p.   cm.
  Originally published: Midland City.
  Includes bibliographical references and index.
  ISBN 0-87389-261-5 (alk. paper)
  1. United States—Economic policy—1993–   2. Total quality
management—United States.   3. Industrial promotion—United States.
4. Municipal government—United States.   I. Title.
  HC106.8.S4   1993
  338.973—dc20   93-4981
                                                            CIP

10987654321

ISBN 0-87389-261-5

Acquisitions Editor: Susan Westergard
Production Editor: Annette Wall
Marketing Administrator: Mark Olson
Set in Avant Garde and Galliard by Linda J. Shepherd.
Cover design by Daryl Poulin. Printed and bound by BookCrafters, Inc.

ASQC Mission: To facilitate continuous improvement and increase customer satisfaction by identifying, communicating, and promoting the use of quality principles, concepts, and technologies; and thereby be recognized throughout the world as the leading authority on, and champion for, quality.

For a free copy of the ASQC Quality Press Publications Catalog, including ASQC membership information, call 800-248-1946.

Printed in the United States of America

    Printed on acid-free recycled paper

 ASQC
Quality Press
611 East Wisconsin Avenue
Milwaukee, Wisconsin 53202

CONTENTS

Midland City is a typical rural community located somewhere in America. The city has lost much of its population base through consolidation of farms. It has lost jobs in the city and is facing a steadily declining economy. In short, either something happens or the city will gradually die.

In most businesses, change is also mandatory. This book began as a story about a single business with varying needs in its several departments. I changed it to a novel about a community to broaden acceptance in the many kinds of organizations.

This book describes how the many departments or parts of any organization must work together or face loss of business and jobs.

This book was written to provide a vision of how a community can shape its destiny and how it can cause the changes that will bring in new jobs and growth.

I wrote *Recovering Prosperity Through Quality: The Midland City Story* as a novel to place characters with names and accomplishments in a context. I felt a book could show how each person in the city (or a business or company) must learn new skills to work together and to solve problems. We need a vision of both the result and the parts that lead to the result.

This book is designed to bring an acceptance of change by everyone in the community as well as to provide a "how to" on the methods and processes for change. Have fun reading and even more fun changing your city.

Change is here. Either we manage it or it manages us.

Robert A. "Bob" Schwarz created the manuscript for *Recovering Prosperity Through Quality: The Midland City Story* in the form of a novel to help create a vision of how quality can be improved. Born in Paynesville, Minnesota, Bob has lived in a number of other rural communities. He serves as a director on two statewide boards for vocational education and as a participant on many committees for productivity and quality improvement. He has been published in magazines and has lectured at numerous conferences.

Formerly an employee of Honeywell, Bob is currently president of Total Quality Systems in Minneapolis. He has a degree in mechanical engineering and extensive training in a wide range of productivity processes. He is past national president of the American Society for Performance Improvement, director of the Minnesota Consortium for Quality and Productivity, and a member of the American Society for Quality Control.

Bob also serves as president of the Board of Directors for the Minnesota Association of Technical Colleges.

The original manuscript was edited by Shelley Beaudry. Shelley has a strong background in newspaper reporting with a focus on business, educational, and local government issues. She has a bachelor of arts degree in newspaper journalism and speech communication from the University of Minnesota.

Together, Bob and Shelley have written a book that creates a compelling vision. Influenced by the effective motivation and leadership of a quality system, your community could benefit from the same success as "Midland City."

A C K N O W L E D G M E N T S

Recovering Prosperity Through Quality: The Midland City Story involved many good friends. They deserve credit for ensuring the accuracy of the examples used. Because of their help, I can be assured that the changes described are all possible. I wanted *Recovering Prosperity Through Quality: The Midland City Story* to be both a source of a vision and a "how to" book providing details.

My thanks to Radcliffe "Buck" Ashworth, Hennepin County; John Robertson, Extensor Corp.; Roger Syverson, Professional Value Services; and Lou Mikunda, Clint Soppeland, and Ted Tammearu, Honeywell for their review of technologies.

Thanks also to my wife, Gloria, for her continuous review and support during preparation.

INTRODUCTION

Recovering Prosperity Through Quality: The Midland City Story incorporates examples of a variety of proven processes for problem solving and data management into a community of people facing failing businesses and job stagnation. My book could just as well have been written about many of our hospitals, banks, or factories. Whichever business I chose, others would have said, "That has nothing to do with me." After a lot of analysis, I wrote it about a community to allow the largest possible audience to gather a vision of the benefits of a commitment to quality.

The total quality management we are pursuing requires a culture that encourages all employees in every organization to solve problems and prevent errors. These new behaviors for generating ideas will require several things.

1. **Management** must understand enough of the possibilities to select goals and choose a path. This book is intended as a tool to provide management a vision of how a wide variety of problem-solving processes could work. The book is recommended as a study guide for successive meetings where ideas on process implementation can be shared and a path chosen.

2. **Training** in new problem-solving skills is necessary for employees to solve problems. As training skills are provided, skill employees reach new skill levels. Training has become a never-ending requirement. The problem is deciding which training and skills will provide the greatest return on investment. *Recovering Prosperity Through Quality: The Midland City Story* is intended to help management and employee teams identify the skills offering the greatest potential.

3. **Rewards** are fundamental to changing behaviors. Some experts challenge the use of rewards as being counter to a team-based organization. This is not true. People seek WIIFM, what's in it for me, in most of life's actions. We have rewards for executives, commissions for salespersons, and bonuses for other workers. To change behaviors, a direct reward for ideas that generate new profits is needed. Suggestion systems and other reward processes are proven in the United States and abroad. Also, successful examples of gain and profit sharing have existed for years.

Please accept the Pollyanna psychology of the book. Certainly, there are numerous examples of failure that I could have included. My choice for a focus on successes was to keep the story short.

Please be assured that there are many failing businesses for each success and that even present success may be doomed to eventual failure without management leadership.

To change your organization to a total quality approach, you must have leadership and patience. Without executive leadership willing to dedicate resources as well as personal time, nothing will get started. Without patience, the changing of behaviors will not have the time to nurture and grow. We did not build the lack of trust and barriers to communication overnight. It will take time and dedication to bring about change.

THE LETTER

It was the best day he'd had in the six years he had been mayor of Midland City, Bill Peterson thought as he rested his feet on the top of his desk. It was a day to celebrate, yet he couldn't feel too relaxed. He and the community still had a lot of work to do.

Earlier in the day just about everyone in Midland City had celebrated at Bingle Park. The high school band played, and the City Quality Program supplied free bratwurst, lemonade, and ice cream for everyone. Bill had proudly unveiled the new signs for the highway leading to Midland City. The signs, stressing the city's pride and dedication to quality, would be posted along with the signs featuring the Midland City Cougars' victory in the 1984 State Boys Basketball Championship.

Even Lieutenant Governor Betty Graham and three state legislators were at the park to share in the celebration. Apex Corporation had chosen Midland City, a city of 8216, as the location for its new electronics plant.

It was a tough fight—plenty of mayors had attempted to lure the Apex plant to their cities, along with the 400 to 600 jobs it would create. But Apex opted for Midland City. Alan Kotch, president of Apex, said it was because Midland City was a fine community where he would be proud to bring his family and one where his company could prosper.

Four years earlier Apex wouldn't have even considered the community in which Bill was born and then went on to raise his family. The thought churned his stomach. At that time Midland City was quietly dying. Sure, Bill and his administrators had put out fires, sobered up drunks, and filled potholes, but the problems weren't so much in appearances as they were in attitudes, economics, and, as much as he hated to admit, leadership.

Welcome to Midland City

8216 People Dedicated to Quality

The Best Schools in the State

Six Outstanding Corporations

The Best Service and Quality from Our
Merchants and Restaurants

Stop and See for Yourself

Welcome to Midland City

Home of the Cougars

1984 State Boys Basketball
Champions

Even his wife, Samantha, had tried to talk him into packing up and moving their son and daughter to the suburbs of Meadan, the state's thriving capital city. "It has an excellent school system where the teachers really seem to care," she had told Bill. "And you could find a job easily. After all, my father is city manager there."

But Bill couldn't leave his hometown of 42 years—not in the shape it was in. Parents, unhappy with the public school system, were transferring their children to St. Paul's Elementary School. Some parents with older children were moving to other communities with better schools. Midland City Bank was foreclosing on numerous farms, businesses on Main Street were closing their doors, and people were either moving to larger cities or living on less income.

Bill knew it was up to him to do something. After all, his late father, Dale Peterson, had been mayor of Midland City 30 years before. Bill wasn't about to let his father's dream die—a dream that Midland City would once again flourish.

And he hadn't, he thought proudly as the telephone rang. It was Samantha.

"Hi, Sam," Bill said to his wife of 20 years.

"When are you coming home?" she asked. "I just got home from picking Scott up from hockey practice, and Sarah just finished cooking dinner. We're waiting for you."

Bill hadn't realized it was already 6:30. Had he been daydreaming that long?

"I'm sorry, honey. I didn't know it was so late. I was just reviewing the letter from Alan Kotch, the president of Apex. And you know what? He wrote that it's an honor to locate his plant here."

"That's wonderful, Bill," Samantha said sincerely. She wondered why she had ever questioned sticking it out in Midland City. At times Bill had been almost unbearable to live with, and often all he could think about was Midland City. But he was dedicated to something he believed in, and she believed in him.

"Can I expect you soon?" she asked.

"Sure. I'll leave as soon as I read Kotch's letter one more time."

In his letter Kotch explained at great length why his company had selected Midland City. He complimented those people who had worked so hard to rebuild the city. The planning, meetings, and hard work had really paid off, Bill thought to himself as he read on:

> The Midland City school system has become one of the best in the state. Its SAT scores and other records of academic achievement, not to mention its athletic programs, are envied by the best schools.

This kind of school performance will draw key technical and management staff with families. And the fact that the school district's curriculum emphasizes statistics and team problem solving assures me that new hires for Apex will be better prepared for our complex challenges.

I commend Midland City School Superintendent Helen Sikorski for her work.

Apex looks forward to hiring many of the fine graduates of your outstanding nearby technical institute and junior college. We at Apex feel the people of Midland City can outperform workers anywhere. They reflect both excellent training and a work-quality attitude unmatched by the other cities we reviewed. We're confident we will not have to spend much time and money training people to do a quality job.

We plan to allow job sharing and offer some seasonal work opportunities for area farmers— a benefit we hope will help keep many of them in business.

Midland's reputation as a "Community of Quality" will greatly benefit Apex when our representatives approach new customers. I respect the way everyone in Midland City has worked together to make theirs the best city in the state, especially how Midland City manufacturers share ideas on how to better manage their plants.

It's impressive how your city established the funds to hire consultants and send 10 representatives to Japan to study its manufacturers' management strategies.

Apex is proud to take part in Midland City's quest for quality. We are looking forward only to success.

Bill liked the attention the media had given him at the picnic that day, he thought as he carefully tucked the letter into his briefcase. Not just any mayor is asked to pose repeatedly for photos with the lieutenant governor. And there had been rumors about his successfully vying for the soon-to-be open senate seat in his district. Why not? Hadn't he provided the vital leadership for his friends?

Bill felt good about being a winner.

Whatever your organization, the kind of letter Bill Peterson read is possible. It is the result of focus on your customers and on satisfying their needs. Here, the customer needs were for a productive work force and a community climate that would be conducive to growth and success. Apex found in Midland City available skilled workers and a community where its executives would be willing to move and raise their families.

A TIME OF TERROR:
FOUR YEARS EARLIER

The call came at about 10:30 on a Friday morning. Bill Peterson had just finished nine holes of golf at the municipal course with Ralph Huber, mayor of Rainville. They played every Friday.

The day had started out badly. Bill double bogied the first hole, tore up the fairway on the last hole, and finished his game with an embarrassing 50, well above his normal four handicap. And after hearing the tone of the police chief's voice, he knew things weren't going to get much better.

"There's been a shooting out at the Braddock farm," said Midland Police Chief Spetch, as he struggled to catch his breath.

Joe Braddock hadn't made a loan payment in many months. Carl Randall, Midland City Bank president, had covered up the delinquent payments as long as he could, but the bank board finally voted to foreclose on Joe's farm.

Joe and his family were devastated by the foreclosure, but Bill never dreamed Joe would resort to such desperate measures. Maybe he would have done something too if his family's livelihood was at stake.

"Randall and the auctioneer both were wounded and have been taken to Midland City Hospital. We have Joe down here at the city jail," Spetch said.

"I'll be right there," Bill said as he grabbed his coat.

A new auctioneer was brought in. By late afternoon Braddock's possessions were sold and the eviction was completed.

A pall of near death hung over Midland City like a thick wet fog enveloping everything in a state of confusion and frustration. No one seemed to know what to do or where to turn.

People they had known all of their lives were turning frustration into violence—a far different breed of violence than the type their beloved Cougars exhibited when they wiped out their opponents on the football field the previous Friday.

Unfortunately, the Braddock sale and foreclosure were typical of the actions that seemed to be happening monthly. The farmers' products brought a return that barely covered the cost of seed, fuel, and chemicals. Their massive debt was the result of an unfavorable national policy coupled with an economy that had disastrously lured many of them to mortgage their precious land to buy machinery. Some farmers blamed the federal government—an entity that seemed much too distant and foreign to bring their troubles. So they directed their anger at the local banker.

But the banker had to minimize his risk. Without payments he could lose the bank. As much as he tried to tell his side of the story, he still became the bad guy—a proverbial catch-22.

Main Street also had its problems. Farmers, its mainstay, were cash poor so each local business sold fewer products and, in turn, had fewer dollars to generate back into the economy. Many of the proprietors were also on the brink of bankruptcy.

Midland City already had lost one implement dealer, one auto dealer, a hardware store, a tavern, and two service stations. Those who lost their jobs either went on welfare or fought for the few jobs left. Thirty-year-old mothers were waitressing, leaving high school girls out of jobs. Neither of Bill's teenagers could get the jobs high school students would normally fill.

Even the dentist had opened a second office in a nearby town to draw enough paying patients to keep his doors open in Midland City.

Bill's auto dealership, one of the more successful businesses in town, also felt the crunch. New car sales hit an all-time low, and repairs and parts sales were up. He was still operating at a profit but couldn't afford to lose much more business.

Clearly, Midland City needed a vision of promise, not one of despair. Something had to change, and fast.

During my business career, I remember many a contract loss that resulted in the kind of anguish that the shooting at the Braddock farm caused. All organizations face traumatic losses. The challenge is to evaluate the cause and select a process to prevent future problems.

THE VISION

Amonth after the Braddock foreclosure Bill attended a meeting in Charles City on economic planning. He found the speaker, Arthur Black, inspiring.

Black talked about communitywide planning and commitment to goals. Those successful in industry, he said, use strategic planning—they establish goals and follow objectives to meet those goals. His message was clear: Communities wanting to thrive had to follow suit.

While all troubled cities basically have the same problems, Black said, thriving ones have the same basic qualities. They have enough jobs for their people, the jobs are insulated from outside forces, and they have benefits that attract families and new industry.

"A wise community sets those qualities as its goals," Black told the attentive audience. "Businesses normally opt for cities that offer tax incentives, have well-educated and dedicated work forces, have reputations for producing quality products, and have good schools and living conditions."

Bill, as well as most of the people at the meeting, was surprised to learn that most of the goals could be achieved without a massive financial investment.

But it couldn't happen overnight, Black said. It would require long hours of hard work and a communitywide commitment.

After the meeting, Bill asked Arthur Black to come to Midland City and speak. Bill was pleased when Black said he would gladly come. Black agreed to July 22, the next city council meeting, a month away.

"You should urge everyone in Midland City to attend the meeting and to participate in the follow-up action," Black advised. "Your success will depend on complete participation."

The next day Bill sent a letter to the city council members. He pondered for nearly an hour before he carefully drafted the letter. He wanted it to be both alarming and convincing.

```
To: All council members
From: Bill Peterson, Mayor

The recent shooting at the Braddock farm should
signal to all of us how critical Midland City's
problems are. In the past year, we have lost six
businesses and 11 farms. Our future is not rosy. It
never will be unless we make some major changes.

    I have arranged for Arthur Black, an outstanding
consultant on community survival, to speak at our
next council meeting on July 22. Mr. Black is con-
vinced change and a bright future is possible for
Midland City.

    I will schedule our next council meeting at the
high school auditorium and will exempt normal busi-
ness. All residents will be invited.

    I'm convinced we must confront the future with a
plan and not wait for the future to deal with us as
it wishes.

    I believe that Arthur Black can help all of us.
```

Bill finished the letter and then telephoned Terry Brand, editor of the *Midland City Press*. She listened to his glowing account of Arthur Black's presentation.

"Sounds like page one material to me," Terry said. "I'll assign a reporter to write a profile of Arthur Black and his vision for Midland City." The story and an editorial urging everyone to attend the meeting would run two days before Black's presentation.

"I'll assign a reporter to cover Black's speech the night of the meeting. I'll be there, too," Terry added.

"Wonderful," Bill said as he leaned back in his chair and gazed out of his second-story window at the empty sidewalks below.

"You know the only way we're going to save our city is to make sure everyone knows how much trouble we're really in, and then let them know how they can help. Since just about everyone in town reads your paper, anything you can print in favor of our cause will surely be appreciated," Bill said as he began to think of other ways to get people involved.

"We don't mind helping as long as there's something newsworthy to report," Terry responded. "And Arthur Black's coming here certainly is."

"I'm glad you agree. Let's keep in touch," Bill said.

"Sounds good," Terry said. "Thanks for the news tip."

Bill called his secretary, Joan, into his office and asked her to start a calling committee to ensure that as many people as possible would attend the meeting

He telephoned Midland City School Superintendent Helen Sikorski and arranged to have Black's speech videotaped. The district had purchased video equipment primarily for taping high school sports events. Using it for something that would benefit the entire city would be an excellent example of how sharing can take place in a community. Also, using the equipment would show those who had deemed the expense a waste of money that it had been a wise investment.

As Bill continued planning the July 22 program, he decided to request the involvement of State Representative Bill Lund. He personally telephoned Lund and was pleased to hear Lund's acceptance.

Bill was excited to go home that night and tell Samantha, Scott, and Sarah of his progress that day. As he drove down Elm, Market, and finally Mark Street, his own block, he counted 15 "For Sale" signs. Bill was convinced that those people would be sorry they bailed out. If they could only wait a few years, they'd also reap the benefits of living in one of the healthiest communities in the country.

Only the most blissful of words described how Bill felt as he ascended the long driveway leading to his 80-year-old, two-story brick home. The trim and porch needed a touch of paint and some of the windows needed to be replaced, but overall the house was in good repair.

The lights were on in the kitchen. Sam or Sarah had started dinner, he thought as he brought his Oldsmobile Regency Ninety-Eight to a halt. He wondered if Sam and the kids would be as enthusiastic as he. Scott and Sarah, of course, would be excited as ever. They loved

Midland City. They knew its every corner like the back of their hands, from the caves down by the river to the swimming quarries on the other end of town where all the kids hung out. All their friends lived in Midland City—friends they never wanted to leave.

Bill hoped Samantha would be excited too. Hadn't she said that if the city was healthy she would love to stay?

"What's for dinner?" Bill asked as he opened the back door.

"Hi, Dad. I've made your favorite—country-fried steak, mashed potatoes, gravy, and fresh green beans from the garden," responded Sarah as she tilted each pan so her father could catch a glimpse of what would soon soothe his hunger pains. Bill had been so wrapped up in his work he had forgotten to take a lunch break.

"Looks scrumptious, Sarah. Where's your mom?"

"Where else but picking up my baby brother from hockey school." Sarah, who had just turned 16 the week before, rolled her eyes in a sign of disgust. "Every time I want the car, mom's got to taxi Scott to this game or that game. You'd think that there was nothing else in this world but hockey. I wanted to go to the library to study for my finals before dinner, but no! When can I get my own car Dad?"

Sarah no more than finished her sentence when Scott walked in. He barely squeezed through the kitchen door with all his equipment. Sweat starting from his matted auburn hair streamed down his perspiration-drenched face.

"What's for dinner, Sis?" he asked.

The stench coming from her younger brother was enough to put her over the edge.

"Nothing, until you take a bath!" she shouted.

"You don't have to yell," Scott responded defensively.

"I'll yell if I want to," Sarah rebutted.

"Stop it, kids. Scott, put your gear away and go clean up. Sarah, you go and help your mother with her bags. I want you all at the dinner table in 15 minutes. I have some good news." Why do teenage siblings always have to fight? Bill asked himself as he poured himself a glass of red wine.

Bill was all smiles during dinner as he told his family of his conversation with Black the night before and of the meeting he was planning.

"Do you really think this Arthur Black can help the city? Haven't things gotten too bad?" asked Samantha, hoping he hadn't detected the sour note in her voice.

"He really believes he can, and so do I," Bill responded.

"Will we still be able to take our trip to Rocky Mountain Park in July?" Samantha asked Bill. "I'm really looking forward to starting my photo essay."

"That's something I forgot to mention," Bill said carefully. He hoped Samantha wouldn't be too upset when he finished breaking the news. "Arthur Black says it's going to take at least one summer of thoughtful planning and at least a year of hard work before we see any apparent changes. I won't be able to take time off this summer. Maybe we can go next summer."

"Does that mean I can sign up for the summer hockey league?" asked Scott excitedly.

"Is that all you can think about?" snapped Sarah.

"Will you kids hush up so your father and I can talk this over," Samantha said as she tried to cool her own temper.

"Can't we try to go in August, or even September?" she asked as she picked at her green beans.

"Well maybe, but for this to work I have to give it my wholehearted effort," Bill said. "Why don't you get involved too, Sam? It's really going to be exciting."

"I'll think about it, but there's not much I can do. My forte is photography, not business."

At least she said she'd think about helping, Bill thought to himself. If he failed to convince Sam of a bright future, who could he convince?

Bill Peterson decided to accept the role of leadership even with the potential for problems. He did what must be done to generate awareness of the possibilities and hopefully involvement of the citizens. Your organization will probably face a more complicated process before you get to the commitment shown in this chapter. There are, however, many examples where executive dedication resulted from just one presentation, just like Bill Peterson hearing Arthur Black. Donald Peterson, President of Ford Motor Company, has stated that the NBC "If Japan Can, Why Can't We?" video was a stimulus for change.

THE TOWN
MEETING

M ore than 2000 people turned out for the meeting in Midland High School's auditorium. There hadn't been so many adults in the school since the basketball play-offs when the Midland City Cougars went on to win the State Basketball Championship.

All six city council members, Representative Lund, and Arthur Black were seated on the stage with Bill. He expected little participation on their part but wanted them visible and in a position indicating their support.

Bill introduced Arthur Black by listing his credentials. "While Arthur Black grew up in a small town and understands small towns, he has an extensive background in industry and is an expert in processes of change," Bill told the receptive group. "He has helped revive many businesses and can adapt the process to communities like ours."

As Black approached the podium, the audience applauded but seemed a bit reserved. Some were wondering what a guy like Black was doing sticking his nose in their town's business.

"First of all, I want to thank you for inviting me to come here tonight," Black said in his opening remarks. "Communities that take action, such as I presume yours is going to do, will rapidly rise above their competition and reestablish their lost economic affluence. 17

Unfortunately, most communities are not like yours and are wallowing in despair rather than initiating change."

Midland City alone couldn't solve the price squeeze problems on its farmers or local manufacturers, Black cautioned, but it could take measures to improve the local economy through a commitment to quality.

With an overhead projector he displayed a brief prayer:

> *God grant me*
> *the serenity*
> *to accept the things*
> *I cannot change*
> *the courage*
> *to change the things*
> *I can*
> *and the wisdom to know*
> *the difference*

"Among the things you 'cannot change' are the basics of American business style," Black told the audience. "Although you can't make things happen on a national basis, you *can* make Midland City successful compared to its neighboring competition because all American communities face the same federal government handicaps."

Black said Midland City could not change the Wall Street mentality that drives industry to seek short-term goals, farm supports that place farm products at an international disadvantage, the United States' thriftless spending habits, and a general national focus on self rather than community.

Black then switched gears and began talking about Japan's business economy with an apology. He said that while he recognized the problems many people have with using examples from Japan, many of Japan's successes are largely the result of U.S. directives.

He told the story of how General Douglas MacArthur had helped Japan become self-sufficient in the late 1940s and early 1960s. In 1946 Japan was a nation reliant on imports for 40 percent of its food, 90 percent of its fuel, and more than 50 percent of its raw material. It had 100 million people, few jobs, and a worldwide reputation for cheap, low quality "Japanese copies."

MacArthur started the change in Japan by recruiting American engineers to establish the manufacturing of radio receivers and telephone products needed to communicate. Two of these engineers were Homer Sarasohn and Charlie Protzman. Sarasohn was responsible for the manufacture of radio receivers and Protzman for telephone equipment.

Homer arrived in late 1945 and quickly found that traditional Japanese management style created excessive numbers of rejects and utilized workers poorly. After Protzman arrived in 1948, they created a unique 250-hour course called "The Fundamentals of Industrial Management" with the focus on the need for quality, capable processes, and leadership principles. The course was required for managers of major Japanese corporations in the area of electronics manufacturing. The trained managers were also required to lead internal groups so they could spread the word. The process worked. Additional courses were planned, but the Korean conflict ended the focus on rebuilding Japan. Sarasohn also wrote the book in Japanese, *The Industrial Application of Statistical Process Control.* Later, in 1950, the well-documented training in statistical process control with Dr. W. Edwards Deming started along with training by Dr. Joseph M. Juran and others.

The Japanese school system, equivalent to our kindergarten through grade 12, was also changed with MacArthur's direction, Black explained. Today, Japanese children spend more hours per day and more days per year in school than American youths. Japanese children have more homework than American students. Further, the Japanese home is very demanding of academic excellence and the support of the parents leads to an ideal learning environment in the schools. The Japanese process causes significant pressure on the youths with their future based on academic achievement at an early age. Black pointed out that this had both good and bad results.

Black continued. He said that our Japanese competitors benefited from the greater worker skills and better work habits. He also noted that meeting Japanese competition was not to be done by mimicking their school process. Black urged Midland City to find ways to get the desired results within their own culture.

During the 1950s and 1960s Japan was seeking ways to build an industrial base, increase job efficiency, and create high-quality products. Deming and Juran were leaders among the consultants brought to Japan. In addition, hordes of Japanese were touring America and Europe to photograph and record work processes. This combination of efforts from researchers and consultants allowed Japan to rapidly train all levels of employees in effective work methods and processes that assured quality.

In this same time frame, American industry had moved from the manufacture of profitable war materials to the production of civilian goods for a largely bombed-out world. The focus of American industries was on profit, and American schools were directed toward letting the baby boomers have some of the good life their parents dreamed of.

Black stated that Midland City needed to learn from others as much as possible. He pointed to the Japanese model of pursuing knowledge through investigative travel and consultants.

Black pointed that some consultants, like Sarasohn, returned to careers in the United States. (Homer was engineering director at IBM.) Others, like Deming and Juran, remained in consulting. The work that Dr. Deming did in Japan led to the establishment of the Deming Award, the prestigious honor for excellence in business.

Dr. Deming developed 14 management principles that have been a guide to excellence for many organizations in the United States. Dr. Juran has alternative principles and other consultants, like Philip Crosby, also have fundamentals that lead to excellence.

Black displayed Deming's 14 principles on the screen, and Bill and some council members passed out copies to the audience.

Black led the audience through the 14 points. He stressed the need to drive out fear in any organization. He pointed to problem solving through teamwork. Each item on the list was discussed.

Black summarized by stating that these were excellent principles and would be a good choice for any organization. He also said that there were also good things to say about the teachings of Juran and Crosby. Black stressed that it is necessary for management to select goals and to choose a path. Black stated that successful organizations eventually incorporate a mixture of the principles from several of the consultants. Continuous improvement and continuous change are the way of the future.

Black then discussed management's problem caused by the wide differences in philosophy and practice between Deming, Juran, and Crosby. These differences place managers in the position of learning many details before committing the business to one or the other.

Black recommended that Midland City managers look to the Malcolm Baldrige National Quality Award for guidelines to effective management principles that were best suited to everyone. He also pointed out that the emergence of the European Common Market had led to the establishment of management and control of processes called ISO 9000. This quality standard creates a control of processes and focus on improvement that is based in Europe and literally sweeping the world. This process would be crucial to any local manufacturers that wanted to sell products in Europe.

Black next presented the details of the Malcolm Baldrige National Quality Award. He pointed out that the Baldrige had become a basic for many organizations. Here again, there is a lack of total acceptance of the Baldrige criteria. Both Crosby and Deming have been negative toward the award and the process it represents. Black pointed out that he personally favored the use of the Baldrige categories to evaluate an organization. He displayed the dynamic relationships of the seven categories of criteria for the audience. The slide showed executive leadership

14 MANAGEMENT PRINCIPLES
by
W. Edwards Deming

1 Create constancy of purpose for improving products and services, allocating resources to provide for long-range needs rather than short-term profitability.

2 Adopt the new philosophy for economic stability by refusing to allow commonly accepted levels of delays, mistakes, defective materials, and defective workmanship.

3 Cease dependence on mass inspection by requiring statistical evidence of built-in quality in both manufacturing and purchasing functions.

4 Reduce the number of suppliers for the same item by eliminating those that do not qualify with statistical evidence of quality: End the practice of awarding business solely on the basis of price.

5 Search continually for problems in the system to constantly improve processes.

6 Institute modern methods of training to make better use of all employees.

7 Focus supervision on helping people do a better job: Ensure that immediate action is taken on reports of defects, maintenance requirements, poor tools, inadequate operating definitions, or other conditions detrimental to quality.

8 Encourage effective, two-way communication and other means to drive out fear throughout the organization and help people work more productively.

9 Break down barriers between departments by encouraging problem solving through teamwork, combining the efforts of people from different areas such as research, design, sales, and production.

10 Eliminate use of numerical goals, posters, and slogans for the work force that ask for new levels of productivity without providing methods.

11 Use statistical methods for continuing improvement of quality and productivity and eliminate work standards that prescribe numerical quotas.

12 Remove all barriers that inhibit the worker's right to pride of workmanship.

13 Institute a vigorous program of education and retraining to keep up with change in materials, methods, product design, and machinery.

14 Clearly define top management's permanent commitment to quality and productivity and its obligation to implement all of these principles.

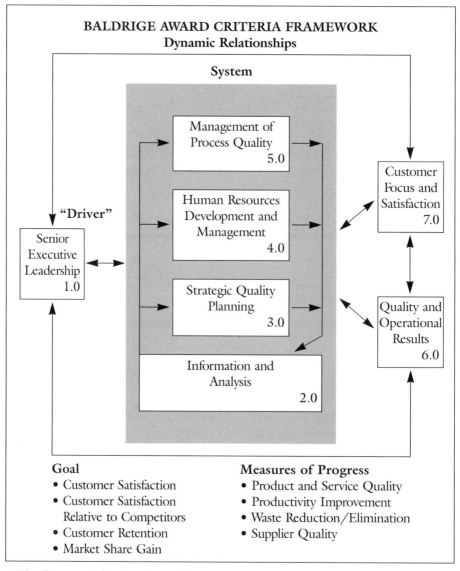

BALDRIGE AWARD CRITERIA FRAMEWORK
Dynamic Relationships

System

Management of Process Quality 5.0

Human Resources Development and Management 4.0

Strategic Quality Planning 3.0

Information and Analysis 2.0

"Driver"

Senior Executive Leadership 1.0

Customer Focus and Satisfaction 7.0

Quality and Operational Results 6.0

Goal
• Customer Satisfaction
• Customer Satisfaction Relative to Competitors
• Customer Retention
• Market Share Gain

Measures of Progress
• Product and Service Quality
• Productivity Improvement
• Waste Reduction/Elimination
• Supplier Quality

The framework has four basic elements.

Driver
Senior executive leadership creates the values, goals, and systems, and guides the sustained pursuit of customer value and company performance improvement.

System
System comprises the set of well-defined and well-designed processes for meeting the company's customer, quality, and performance requirements.

Measures of Progress
Measures of progress provide a results-oriented basis for channeling actions to delivering ever-improving customer value and company performance.

Goal
The basic aim of the quality process is the delivery of ever-improving value to customers.

BALDRIGE AWARD CATEGORY SUMMARIES

1.0 Leadership—Examines senior executives personal leadership and involvement in creating and sustaining a customer focus and clear and visible quality values. Also examines how the quality values are integrated into the company's management system and reflected in the manner in which the company addresses its public responsibilities and corporate citizenship.

2.0 Information and analysis—Examines the scope, validity, analysis, management, and use of data and information to drive quality excellence and to improve operational and competitive performance. Also examines the adequacy of the company's data, information, and analysis system to support improvement of the company's customer focus, products, services, and internal operations.

3.0 Strategic quality planning—Examines the company's planning process and how all key quality requirements are integrated into overall business planning. Also examines the company's short- and long-term plans and how quality and operational performance requirements are deployed to all work units.

4.0 Human resources development and management—Examines the key elements of how the work force is enabled to develop its full potential to pursue the company's quality and operational objectives. Also examines the company's efforts to build and maintain an environment for quality excellence conducive to full participation and personal and organizational growth.

5.0 Management of process quality—Examines the systematic process the company uses to pursue ever-higher quality and company operational performance. Examines they key elements of process management, including research and development, design, management of process quality for all work units and suppliers, systematic quality improvements, and quality assessment.

6.0 Quality and operational results—Examines the company's quality levels and improvement trends in quality, company operational performance, and supplier quality. Also examines current quality and operational performance levels relative to those of competitors.

7.0 Customer focus and satisfaction—Examines the company's relationships with customers and its knowledge of customer requirements and of the key quality factors that drive marketplace competitiveness. Also examines the company's methods to determine customer satisfaction, current trends and levels of customer satisfaction and retention, and these results relative to competitors.

working through four categories to yield operational results and customer satisfaction.

With the help of Bill Peterson and the others seated on the stage, Black distributed copies of the relationship figure and summaries of the seven categories of criteria.

After everyone had their copies, Black noted that these seven summaries are copied from the 1993 Baldrige guidelines. He said that in a Baldrige evaluation, 300 of the possible 1000 points are awarded for category 7.0, customer focus and satisfaction. Black put up a screen showing the address for obtaining a copy of the Baldrige award criteria and urged each business to use them as a part of its planning. Black also pointed out that the American Society for Quality Control (ASQC) was a resource for Baldrige materials and support.

Black explained that what he had been doing was a form of benchmarking—gaining an understanding of available choices. He said he wanted to explain some relationships in his own way.

"With this slide, we have moved into what Midland City can do," Black told the audience. "Any change process that Midland City uses should incorporate these principles.

"Let's look at what management must do," Black said as he pointed to the transparency. It listed the inputs, outputs, and manageable items

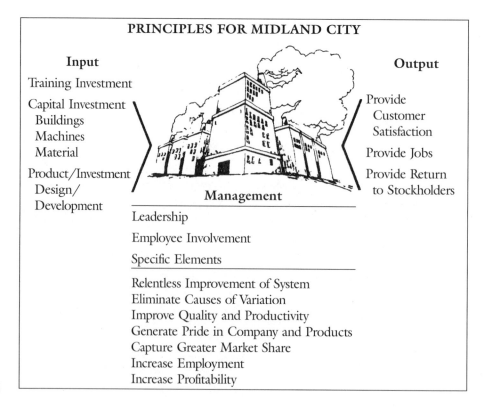

PRINCIPLES FOR MIDLAND CITY

Input
Training Investment
Capital Investment
  Buildings
  Machines
  Material
Product/Investment
  Design/
  Development

Output
Provide
Customer
Satisfaction
Provide Jobs
Provide Return
to Stockholders

Management
Leadership

Employee Involvement

Specific Elements

Relentless Improvement of System
Eliminate Causes of Variation
Improve Quality and Productivity
Generate Pride in Company and Products
Capture Greater Market Share
Increase Employment
Increase Profitability

of a factory. He discussed each of the steps management must take for improvement.

Relentless Improvement of the System

The businesses in Midland City should not sell anything of low quality. They should sell only quality products. Black went on to explain that they need to improve production methods by constantly using statistical measures, team problem solving, and other quality improvement processes.

Eliminate Causes of Variation

Businesses must use statistical data to identify the causes of variation that hinder product quality. Management should lead the company into continuous improvement of product by reducing variation. American farmers are longtime practitioners of this concept. They reduce the variation in yield between plots of land or different dairy cows as much as possible. By reducing variance, farmers cause each acre of land or each cow to produce the most possible.

Improve Quality and Productivity

Black explained that quality and productivity are inseparable. When a company increases quality it automatically increases productivity. Measuring quality compared to productivity is relatively easy and provides a base for relentless improvement.

Generate Pride

"The pride generated in a Japanese company is outstanding and something that Midland City should duplicate," Black said. "A Japanese company establishes its goals so that its employees take pride, and the company reinforces that pride by acknowledging and rewarding its employees for their accomplishments."

Capture Greater Market Share

"Management must lead the company in the proper direction of product development and investment that will capture a greater share of the market, and as a result, build jobs and promotion opportunities. Midland City must capture a larger share of new businesses. It must offer benefits beyond the competition."

Increase Employment

"Japanese companies are always looking for ways to create new jobs. So should Midland City," Black said. "It should always be looking at ways to lure new companies and encourage expansion of existing ones."

Increase Profitability

"Any changes management makes must ultimately increase profitability. This is the bottom line," Black said. "Experience, both here and abroad, proves that these initiatives will result in increased profits."

Black removed the transparency and switched off the overhead projector. He repeated the urgent need for change. "Midland City must establish a plan of action that includes training for everyone, quality measurements to use, a way to involve employees in management, and reward and recognition programs for employees," he said.

On an easel, he listed a number of quality control processes that are widely used in Japan and in some U.S. companies. He explained that they were the processes Midland City would use.

- Statistical process control
- Team problem solving (quality circles)
- Suggestion systems
- Work flow analysis
- Value analysis
- Design of experiments

Black noted that the list was far from complete, but it was complete enough to keep everyone busy for a few years.

Bill watched the audience carefully. Black was a bit tutorial but inspiring. At least he had the attention of the best informed and, fortunately, no one seemed to be nodding off.

"We all need to know how to use statistics," Black continued, "but our schools are not adequately preparing us to apply them to all jobs to measure both quality and productivity.

"Midland City needs statistics to set goals, solve problems, and work toward quality in a logical manner," Black stressed.

He suggested a strategic plan by which Midland City could focus community effort and establish priorities.

"Your goal is to return Midland City to a level of economic affluence equal to or greater than four years ago. Is that right?" he asked. Members of the audience nodded their heads in agreement.

"To do this you must increase the disposable incomes of farmers, increase industry payrolls, increase tourism, and bring in new manufacturing and service industry.

"Your plan must include means that are in your power. And what is in your power is creating quality products and a quality community environment," Black said.

"Each person, each organization, and each company must focus on the quality of his or her product, whether that product be a completed homework assignment, a lesson plan, a business letter, the steel a salesperson provides a machinist, the parts a machinist provides an assembler, the product an assembler ships to the merchant, or what the merchant sells to the customer.

"Product is exchanged between husbands and wives, clergy and congregations. In short, 'product' is what is between all people who interact.

"Whenever we receive product we want it to be right. We must, in turn, be just as concerned about the product we provide to others," he said.

Black described his vision of a community where the high school students' Standard Achievement Test (SAT) scores were the best in the state, where the industries worked together to build an image where only quality products were produced, and where the restaurants, service stations, and hospitals all cared that they provided fast and error-free service.

"Such a community would become a magnet for new businesses and insurance for the success of existing businesses. You can be that community!" he said as he slammed the lectern with his fist for emphasis.

Change, Black stressed, would take work and commitment and at least one year before results could be measured. "Your alternative," he warned, "is to wallow in despair and watch a fine community deteriorate and slowly die."

Black closed the presentation by praising Bill for having enough courage to expose Midland City to scrutiny, planning, and change.

"You owe Mayor Peterson a great deal of thanks. He truly loves your city and is willing to sacrifice to make it one of the best cities in the nation and reestablish its life-style."

The Midland City residents applauded mildly. They appeared a little dazed and overwhelmed. Bill rose and announced a 20-minute break with coffee and cookies in the lunchroom. He urged those interested in participating in the planning process to return to the auditorium after the break.

Conversation during the break began slowly. Gradually, however, it heightened to a productive level. Bill was pleased to hear most people

talking about the speech. He hoped that most would choose to participate rather than go home. "Midland City needs a real boot in the butt
if it's going to change," Bill commented to his neighbor, Bob Hendrix,
during the break.

To Bill's surprise, nearly everyone returned to the auditorium. Most
of those who left had gone home to relieve their baby-sitters.

Bill opened the discussion first to remarks by the council members.

"This is the best idea I've heard in a long time," said council member Sybil Hensley. "I'd like to start planning right away."

"But is everyone going to be willing to share in the work? Everyone
already has a job," complained council member Fred Johnson. If anyone
was going to be a pessimist about change, Johnson was the person, Bill
thought to himself.

"And what about the manufacturers? Will they trust each other
enough to be able to work together?" Johnson continued.

"I'm willing to try," said council member Dean Ostman, owner of
Midland City Manufacturing.

"We have no choice. We have to do something. If Mayor Peterson
thinks this is best, we ought to try it," shouted Police Chief Spetch from
the audience. "We need to do something to stop foreclosures and shoot-
ings," he added.

"I agree," yelled several people in the audience.

After nearly an hour of discussion, Sybil Hensley moved to establish
a plan. "I guess I feel the strategic plan Black outlined is as close to our
needs as we could get. Bill has bounced it off many of us during the past
two weeks and we all seem to agree it could work in our community."

Council member Ostman seconded the motion and it passed
unanimously.

"I would like to get things started. We don't have time to waste," Bill
said. "However, we can't go down blind alleys either. I suggest we set up
committees that include community members to work on the strategic
plan, to further define what Midland City's problems are, and to start a
training program.

Bill recommended that the city hire consultants, including Arthur
Black, to assist in the planning and training.

Bill assigned each council member to lead one of six committees:
Angus Taylor would be in charge of increasing spendable farm income;
Sybil Hensley would work on increasing industry payroll; Wayne
Dietrich would work on increasing tourism; Dean Ostman would work
to bring in new manufacturing industry; Fred Johnson would work to
bring in new service industry; and Susan Anderson would develop a
training program.

"I'll lead a seventh group that will include a representative from each of our five local manufacturers. Our objective will be to pursue quality jointly," Bill said.

Bill urged the audience members to sign up for the committee of their choice. Each committee would have one meeting within two weeks and all would participate in a day-long strategic planning session in four weeks. Fred Johnson agreed to share details of the meetings with everyone through the *Midland City Press*.

The meeting lasted until nearly midnight. Bill wondered what Samantha would say about his coming home so late. She had declined his invitation to the town meeting because she said she had too many other things to do. His wife would understand after he told her how successful the meeting had gone, Bill reassured himself.

This chapter shows how a consultant can combine a benchmarking function and a role of leadership toward defining change. Too often the internal leadership is questioned for the thoroughness of its analysis and, as a result, the accuracy of its vision. Here, the consultant served the purpose of educating and leading the group to a plan and action. There was still the presence and commitment of the mayor, Bill Peterson, assuring that the decisions would be carried out.

In many businesses, leadership by the owner or the top executive is effectively supported with consultants. The key to success is dedicated internal leadership coupled with expert knowledge of the options and a clear selection of both goals and the path to achieve them.

THE COSTS
OF NONQUALITY

Bill was surprised to find Samantha waiting up for him. She was in her darkroom drying the photographs she had taken earlier in the evening.

"It's late," she commented as he entered the doorway.

"The meeting was well worth it," Bill responded. "Are you interested in hearing about it?"

"Sure, but I don't want to stay up too much later. I have to get up early tomorrow morning to take Scott to hockey school."

"Speaking of Scott," Bill responded quickly, "we have to have a serious talk with him about his aspirations in life. He doesn't seem to realize that there is more to life than hockey."

"Stop right there, Bill!" Samantha snapped. "Scott's one of the star hockey players on his team. He's worked hard to get where he is. He's only 13."

"That's just it, Sam. He works hard, but only at hockey. He just barely passed the eighth grade with Cs and Ds."

"He's trying, but he has practice almost every day," Samantha said.

"I think we ought to have him cut down on hockey and concentrate more on school. He has to realize that to succeed in life he must excel in many areas and use his talents to their fullest. That's what Black talked about tonight—well not about Scott, but about how everyone in a community must work to his or her potential."

Samantha, anticipating a lecture, folded her arms and dropped into the chair behind her.

Bill briefed Samantha on what he had learned at the town meeting

"Do you know that most American manufacturers waste over 20 percent of their operating dollars in the form of scrap, salvage, reruns, retyping, and corrected analyses in the office? And 80 percent of those wasted costs are caused by system problems or from errors by engineers, managers, and administrators."

"What does all that have to do with Scott?" Samantha asked.

"Maybe as managers of Scott's development, we've erred by letting him concentrate so much on hockey," Bill said trying to draw a parallel that Samantha at first failed to buy.

"That's ridiculous. Scott's not a factory. He's a young boy who is enjoying what he likes to do," Samantha said defensively.

"That's just it. Just by us not saying anything, we have led him to believe that it's okay not to try to excel at a number of things.

"Our manufacturers have done the same thing," Bill said as he continued to equate Black's talk with his own family's situation. "They've ignored the fact they're cost inefficient and continue on with the status quo."

As Black pointed out, Bill continued, to get people to take the risks that change entails, there has to be either a threat or an incentive.

"Nobody wants to stick his neck out if there isn't a reason. Just like Scott. By playing hockey, he gets the immediate reward of praise from his teammates, friends, and us. Maybe he hasn't worked hard in school because we haven't shown him the rewards or the consequences of doing so.

"What happens if he doesn't get a hockey scholarship? Will he still want to go to college, and will he be willing to help us pay his tuition?" Bill asked.

Samantha began to catch on. "Maybe you'll have to talk with him. I don't think I'm the person to do it. When I was in school all I was interested in was photography and I did okay," she said.

"Even if Scott does get a scholarship, what are the chances he'll make the pros? How would he make a living? Photography is different," Bill pointed out. "We both need to talk to him, Sam. If only one of us does, he'll think that only one of us is picking on him and he'll go running to the other for shelter. What do you say?"

"I'll think about it," said Samantha as she headed for bed. Bill followed her thinking that changing Scott's attitude, as well as most everyone's attitude in Midland City, was going to be quite a challenge.

As Bill lay in bed he almost began to dread the days ahead. Changing Midland City would take a lot of his time and would stretch his limited staff and budget. But there must be a change and Midland City needed his leadership.

Bill knew he had to convince the manufacturers to fully understand and adopt Deming's 14 principles and/or the Baldrige Award guides. He also wanted them to measure the cost of quality as proposed by Philip Crosby. Measuring all of the costs associated with poor quality would provide the manufacturers with the vision of how much they actually could save.

The process to evaluate the costs of quality was really quite simple, and the results could be a powerful persuader toward spending time and money in support of change. The next day, Bill proceeded to draft a letter to the manufacturers committee.

To: Manufacturers Committee
From: Bill Peterson

Subject: Cost of Quality

We need a way to identify the waste caused by poor quality in each organization.

I want each of you to go through the following steps. It would be helpful if you included a number of your staff in the analysis to gain a larger sample. This analysis should only take about one-half hour.

Step 1—Everyone list what they do during a typical day. Keep lists to under 20 items if possible. Keep the list on the left side of a typical tablet page. You may want to provide a form with the columns already there (see attached example). Only title the first column so your employees do not anticipate the next question.

Step 2—In the first column, enter the amount of time you spend each day on each work item. Enter this figure as a percent of your total work time. For example, if you had 10 work items and spent the same amount of time on each one, then you would enter 10 percent for each work item.

ACTIVITIES LIST FOR COST OF QUALITY

Activity	% of Time	% of Doing Work	% of Doing Prevention	% of Correcting Failure
Teach Classes	40	70 / 28	15 / 6	15 / 6
Attend Meetings	15	33 / 5	33 / 5	33 / 5
Answer Phones	5	60 / 3		40 / 2
Contact Students	5	20 / 1	80 / 4	
Plan Classes	35	60 / 21	30 / 10.5	10 / 3.5
Total	100%	58	25.5	16.5

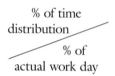

% of time distribution / % of actual work day

Step 3—In the second column, for each work item, estimate how your efforts are expended using the categories shown. The estimates for each work item should total 100 percent. For example, for one work item you might spend 50 percent of your time on meaningful work, 25 percent of your time on preventing errors, and 25 percent of your time on correcting errors.

Meaningful work—This is when usable output is generated.

Preventing errors—Inspection, training, and proofreading are examples of trying to prevent errors.

Correcting errors—Retyping letters, throwing out excess food, scrapping or salvaging materials, and similar activities are examples of correcting errors.

Step 4—Now multiply the figures in the first column (% of Time) by the percentages in each of the last three columns and enter the number (% of Total) under the diagonal line.

This analysis allows each of us to evaluate the cost of errors in our business. The cost of errors or failure in the example is only 16.5 percent. Typically, an organization will find numbers between 20 percent and 35 percent. The percent assigned to errors usually increases as skill in the cost of quality (COQ) process grows.

The 16.5 percent is enough to cause a focus on the need to eliminate errors to increase competitive position or customer satisfaction.

Please bring a summary similar to the sample to the meeting on Saturday.

The use of a COQ measure is very effective. Our businesses are profit driven and dollar measures are the only way to get management's attention. We are also reluctant to change processes or plans if we are satisfied that they are working well and leading us in the right direction. COQ is one way to focus on the monetary impact of errors and thus allows budgets to support change.

THE
MANUFACTURERS

The manufacturers arrived at 9:00 A.M. on Saturday in the conference room at Bill's dealership. They all seemed enthused. Some already had met earlier for breakfast at Evan's Diner to discuss their presentations.

Arthur Black opened the meeting by asking them to state their attitudes toward change and whether they believed improving the quality of their products was the key to Midland City's success.

Black, pleased with the responses, restated his belief that changing Midland City would involve four steps.

An imperative—Everyone must recognize a sufficient threat or benefit from change.

A vision—Everyone must understand the benefits of change. They must know what is in it for themselves or their businesses.

The process—Everyone must learn how to use the tools, procedures, and processes needed to achieve the results understood in the vision.

The plan—Everyone must agree on what steps would be used, when the steps would be taken, and who would take them to make the vision a reality.

Midland City already had made progress toward defining and publicizing its vision. During the strategic planning meeting a week later, Midland City residents would define the processes and plans they would use, Black said.

"I want all of you to leave this meeting with a full understanding of the need to push for quality work," he said.

Black subdivided the manufacturers into small groups and asked each group to determine what the cost of quality would be for each of their members. It took them nearly an hour to compile the data they had brought with them.

COST OF QUALITY DATA

Office and Technical Management	Total Percent of Time	Percent of Time Doing the Job	Percent of Time Preventing Errors	Percent of Time Correcting Failure
Staff meetings	10	5	5	
Customer meetings	5		1	3
Shop problem meetings	15			15
Data analyses	5	5		
Schedule reviews	5		2	3
Bid reviews	10	7	3	
Order signing and reviews	10	7	4	
Training	10	5	5	
Employee counseling	10	10		
Planning	10	5	5	
Community relations	10	10		
Total	**100%**	**54%**	**25%**	**21%**

Dave Barker, director of manufacturing for Midland City Machine, was the first to present that company's data on office and technical management to the entire group. "I have never looked at my operation in this fashion, and I was shocked by the waste of labor and materials in every department," he told his group members as he presented his data on a flip chart.

Dave's group members determined that Midland City Machine's cost of quality was the sum of the percent of time it spent preventing errors plus the percent of time correcting errors. They found that his employees wasted an average of 46 percent of their time being nonproductive.

Black interrupted Dave immediately. "All costs of prevention cannot be identified as waste. Certainly poorly planned or excessive training could be argued as waste instead of prevention. Also, inspection functions can be partly prevention and partly waste depending on their effectiveness." Dave nodded and said that he understood the subtle definition that was required and that all prevention was not waste.

Dave anticipated that when he shared this data with his office and technical managers they would be reluctant to admit that their waste ratios were probably higher than the shop's waste ratio.

As the other manufacturers shared their data, they found they all had costs of nonquality above 20 percent.

"You have to shift from correction to prevention and concentrate on finding the real cost for each error, and then eliminate it," Black explained. "There are a number of ways that you can find and correct causes of error."

Black asked the manufacturers to brainstorm for a few minutes and then list what they perceived as their major problems and causes of error. While they represented different styles of business, they had many of the same problems of quality as well as the same causes of error.

"That's not uncommon," Black reassured them. "You are all wasting up to 40 percent of your resources."

The manufacturers had a few remaining comments and questions.

"I wonder just how committed management will be when the process is started," said Harold Leaf, plant supervisor at Midland City Tool and Die.

"I'm worried about our office workers," said Marian Jones, office manager at Midland City Machine. "I doubt that they'll be able to relate to all of this. They'll probably view this as another program doomed for failure."

"We're going to need a finance system to measure the cost of quality," Dean Ostman added.

Black assured them that with proper training and long-term planning, and commitment to those plans, they would reap the benefits of their efforts.

"You need to start to learn the processes for measuring performance and identifying causes of error," Black explained. "I urge you to visit selected companies that have successfully implemented change."

Black adjourned the meeting with his promise to help arrange some plant visits.

Arthur Black attempted to make sure that the manufacturers understood the finer points of COQ. Splitting work elements into meaningful work, prevention, and waste were not simple tasks. Black attempted to show that even when doing meaningful work, there were probable elements of waste through poor tools, materials, processes, or designs. To refine the COQ data would take time and skill.

When using the cost of quality for the first time, I have found it easiest to keep the definitions simple and complexity low. The usual objective of a first meeting is to get everyone's attention and commitment and even a cursory COQ process does that. Plan on further refinements in subsequent meetings. It is also desirable to assign a study committee to come up with COQ rules for future use. This generates ownership of the process.

COQ should not be used as an absolute measure. There are too many variables of interpretation that make month-to-month comparisons dangerous. It is an excellent measure of the big picture and can be used to show trends and to prioritize resource investments.

THE TALK

Sunday morning after church Bill and Samantha asked Scott and Sarah to join them in the family room. Bill had thought long and hard about what he would say. Samantha had too. They were a bit nervous about how Scott would react, but it was something they had to do.

Bill started: "Scott, your mother and I are worried about you. We think you may be spending too much time on hockey and not enough on your grades. We know you are capable of doing much better in school."

"But Dad, my grades weren't that bad last year. I passed didn't I?" Scott became impatient and started to grind his teeth and roll his eyes as he always did when he felt threatened. "Don't you want me to do good in hockey?"

"Yes we do, honey," responded Samantha. "But your father and I feel you are much more capable than that. We want you to go to a good college and —."

"And what? Be a mayor and a car dealer like Dad? Forget it! I want to play hockey with the pros."

"With an attitude like that you'll never make it, Scott," Bill said. He was proud of how supportive his wife had become in the matter, but disappointed in his son's reaction.

"To make it in this world, you have to at least try in everything you do. If you don't, you're going to be known as a quitter," Bill explained.

"I'm not a quitter. I've made mistakes in hockey, and I've always come back and scored." Scott had tears in his eyes.

Everyone felt the tension in the room. Scott was confused. He thought his parents were proud of him, but he was starting to wonder. Bill was angry with Scott who he felt was unwilling to try to understand. Sarah was becoming increasingly impatient; she was 10 minutes late for her date. Samantha was worried a family quarrel was brewing which would evolve into a silent war.

Bill firmly took charge of the family meeting. "We know you're a good hockey player and someday you may be a great one. But if you want to be drafted by the pros, you have to show how well you can play in college. And to get into a college where you will be noticed you need good grades."

"But . . ."

"No buts, Scott, that's a fact," Bill said.

Scott crossed his arms and reclined, slamming his back into the couch. He knew he wasn't going to get in another word.

"Your mother and I have spent a lot of money and energy on your hockey, and we know that it has been a good investment. But we want to spend our money and energy on your education too. You still have plenty of time to bring your grades up," Bill said. "We have decided to hire a tutor to help you catch up. If our community makes the changes we are planning at Midland City High School, you're going to need the help.

"Sarah will help you with your studies, too," Samantha added.

"I don't have the time to help him, Dad. I have my own work to do. When will I be able to see my friends?" Sarah protested.

"Helping Scott won't take that much of your time," Bill reassured his daughter. Sixteen-year-olds sure are selfish with their time, he thought to himself.

"Scott, we want you to keep track of the number of hours you spend on hockey and the number of hours you spend with your tutor and studying," Bill told his son. "Since we agree that hockey is important and something you enjoy, we want you to keep playing. But we want you to spend twice as much time studying as you do playing hockey until we see some improvement in your grades. Once you bring your grades up to a B average, you can spend an equal amount of time on both."

"We want to make this a family affair. We want to help you, but first you have to help yourself," Samantha added.

Scott agreed halfheartedly for the sake of being excused.

Sarah, thankful that she hadn't been the topic of discussion, hurried off to meet her date.

Bill and Samantha looked at each other after their children left the room and shrugged their shoulders.

"Do you think this will really work?" asked Samantha dubiously.

"I don't know, but it's a start in the right direction," Bill responded.

They remained in the family room for the entire afternoon playing Scrabble and watching golf on television. Bill knew he had a lot of work to do for Midland City, but he also needed some quality time with his wife and was glad he took it.

As Bill lay in bed that night, he wondered whether he had been fair in requiring Sarah to help her brother. Maybe he'd buy her a used car for helping Scott. A car would make the task more palatable and fair, he decided.

Bill identified that Scott's long-range goals might not be well established. He used a family team approach to define Scott's study schedule to improve poor grades and made arbitrary assignments for Sarah. This is not a pretty example of team problem solving or conflict resolution. It is an example of benevolent dictator of parent-child management.

It would have been better if Bill had first collected from Scott his goals before presenting management objectives. Also, Sarah could have been asked what help she could or would provide and made the acquisition of a car a negotiation instead of a unilateral reward. Bill lost valuable ownership of his process through his management style.

THE STRATEGIC
PLANNING MEETING

A month after Arthur Black's presentation at the city council meeting, more meetings, letters, phone calls, and conversations had taken place than anyone had imagined.

At their August meeting the city council members had tailored Black's strategic plan suggestions to fit the community's overall goal, which was to return Midland City to its level of affluence of four years earlier. They would do that by increasing their farmers' incomes with part-time employment opportunities in industry, by promoting economic growth of local manufacturers, by convincing manufacturers and merchants to provide only quality products and services, by recruiting new manufacturing and service industries, and by training everyone in at least two key processes—team problem solving and statistical process control.

To process the mass of ideas flowing about the community, the council members decided to adopt Midland City Machine's suggestion system on a citywide basis. But they faced the perennial problem of money, or rather the lack of it. They needed a substantial amount of money immediately to pay for the trainers, travel, books, and publicity. Changing the city's tax base, which would take months or years to set up, was not the answer.

The council members decided to recommend at the planning meeting that local merchants and manufacturers with payrolls pay a 1 percent gross sales tax. The 1 percent tax would yield more than $20,000 a month, enough to pay for trainers and to cover publicity costs.

They would suggest that the city also assess the businesses 10 percent of their profit from additional sales they gained due to the communitywide effort on quality. The 1 percent gross sales tax would be phased out as the 10 percent contribution on gains met budgets.

Bill had mentioned the idea to some of the merchants and manufacturers before the planning meeting. Many opposed the idea, but when Bill asked for alternative suggestions, they grudgingly admitted they had no others.

Bill opened the strategic planning meeting by asking representatives from each of the six committees to report their findings. Each representative exceeded his or her allocated 15 minutes, but Bill, even though he despised long meetings, allowed them to do so. The enthusiasm was too valuable to intervene. Bill was pleased with how everyone saw the need to work for quality in everything.

"Anything that isn't done correctly must be done again and the costs of redoing are wasted," said Lisa Ryner, owner of Midland Bakery. "Therefore, quality is basic for bakers, secretaries, mechanics, factory workers, and everyone. All of us provide a product. It should be right the first time."

Ryner raised a sign carrying the slogan that her committee, charged with increasing tourism, had designed for Midland City. "Quality Is the Key to Our Future," she read aloud.

The slogan brought applause and whistles of approval.

"It's obvious that Midland City will not be able to reach its goal all at once," Bill said as he regained control of the meeting. "For the first year I suggest we cultivate a citywide suggestion system, start training in team problem solving through quality circles and task teams, and train everyone, at different levels of course, in statistical analysis techniques."

"I'll accept nominations for people to head the suggestion system after the meeting," Bill said. The job would be full-time and would include coordinating publicity.

Bill outlined the council's funding proposal. Some of the merchants were convinced the 1 percent tax would drive customers out of town, but most said the plan was a reasonable way to raise money and would generate loyalty—a sign of working together to help each other.

Council member Susan Anderson then suggested the ideas her committee members had for a training program. They recommended that a core group of Midland City's representatives use the nearby technical institute's training package in team problem solving based on early work in quality circles. The core group would then train others who were interested.

"Some of our larger area corporations could help mentor this process," she suggested. "One representative should join the Association for Quality and Participation and become the town professional.

Quality circles, Susan explained, are small groups of employees or people with a common area of interest and expertise, who meet regularly to identify and analyze problems, and recommend and often carry out solutions. The concept is built on the assumption that often the best people to identify and solve problems are those who are directly affected by those problems.

Quality improvement teams (QIT) have replaced circles in most organizations. The QIT is established to solve a specific problem where circles are ongoing for the members.

Training in *statistical process control* is available from a number of sources, Susan further explained. "We recommend using either the technical institute or the community college. Both offer the course 'Transformation of American Industry' developed by Jackson Community College in Michigan which was promoted by the auto industry."

Bill then reported what had happened during his meetings with the manufacturers. He outlined their plans to work together on management techniques and still retain proprietary product protection.

"The management of our five local manufacturers have agreed that once Midland City is known for quality products, both business volume and unit profit will improve," he said.

They had established a "Monday Club" and would meet every Monday at noon at Tom's Cafe to share their plans and results.

School Superintendent Helen Sikorski said that as part of the strategic plan she intended to emphasize academic excellence by establishing new tough rules. She handed out copies of her proposed changes.

- All students will be required to meet established skill levels in reading, writing, and math before they can move up a grade.

- Participation in athletics or other after-school activities will be permitted only for students with a C average or better in all courses.

- Academic achievements will be publicized in the *Midland City Press.*

- Students' SAT scores must be improved.

- Parental support must be gained for all of these changes.

FIRST-YEAR TIMETABLE
DAYLONG PLANNING COMMITTEE

Task	1	2	3	4	5	6	7	8	9	10	11	12
Team Problem Solving												
Train Steering Committee		////										
Train Leaders			////	////	////							
Train Members					////	////	////	////	////	////	////	////
Operate Teams					////	////	////	////	////	////	////	////
Statistical Process Control												
Train Steering Committee		////										
Train Trainers			////	////	////							
Problem Solving/Data Use						////	////	////	////	////	////	////
School Curricula												
Use New Curricula						////	////	////	////	////	////	////
School SAT Focus												
Planning	////	////	////									
Implementation				////	////	////	////	////	////	////	////	
Measured Results											////	////
Suggestion System												
Train Administrators			////	////								
Implement					////	////	////	////	////	////	////	////

Today   Months

After Helen finished her presentation, Bill handed out a yearlong timetable for the several tasks involved in training, changes in school, and the suggestion system.

Bill suggested to Helen that she work with Susan Anderson to search for training in statistical process control and team problem solving. Helen agreed that they would have to work quickly to establish the training skills in Midland City schools.

Bill volunteered to experiment with those processes in his auto dealership. He knew he needed to provide an example from the retail area. Weeks ago, Arthur Black had told Bill to take a strong leadership role in the processes. Black said the leadership would provide Bill with both political and technical advantages.

Bill shared the results of his discussions with the manufacturers and businesses regarding the other processes Arthur Black had identified. Bill was pleased to report that each of the processes was set for a trial by one of the businesses.

Midland City Machine would work with *value engineering/value analyses,* commonly referred to as *value analyses.* The company designed and manufactured an extensive line of power woodworking tools. Company President Pete Ivers said the process could help improve his product design.

Trock Plastics would work with *design of experiments.* Trock produced a variety of products, primarily injection moldings to customers' designs. It also had a line of plastic garbage bags sold under a variety of labels. John Trock said the many variables in his manufacturing processes would benefit from experimental design techniques.

Midland City Fulfillment would use *work flow analysis/work simplification.* The company handled coupon redemption for a number of manufacturers located in the city. It printed refund checks and shipped mail order merchandise. Company President Carol Postman said she was eager to identify the best operating layout to reduce warehouse and office operating costs.

A *cause-and-effect diagram* is essential to determine precisely where wasted costs occur, Bill said. As Arthur Black had suggested, Bill showed the group how the diagram works by drawing one on an easel as a way to summarize the strategic planning meeting.

"The diagram is also referred to as a fishbone diagram," Bill explained. "It was first used by Kaoru Ishikawa in Japan in the 1940s. It will help us outline the causes of poor quality."

Bill felt confident as he drew the diagram on the flip chart. Black had shown him several times how to do it.

"We have established our ideas and plans based on the standard approach to problem solving. However, by doing this, we may have

CAUSE-AND-EFFECT DIAGRAM

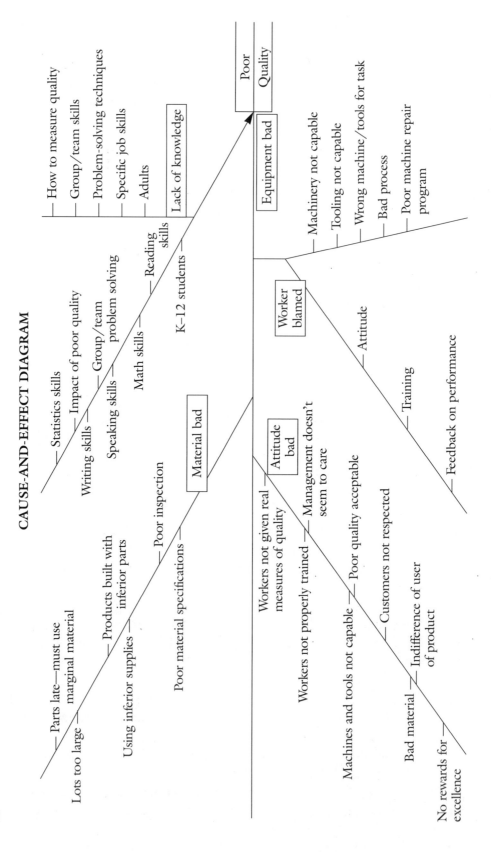

ignored important points and interactions between those points," Bill explained.

Bill asked the group to take five minutes and think of every cause of poor quality they had experienced, knew of, or could imagine in Midland City. After five minutes, he asked each person to offer one idea and he listed the ideas on a flip chart in sequence around the table.

After consolidating those ideas closest in concept, he arranged them according to lack of knowledge and training, inefficient equipment and tools, poor materials and supplies, and bad attitudes. The causes all led up to bad quality.

He wrote *poor quality* on the right of the chart and then he led the group to arranged the causes and their effects according to category.

"We must keep this diagram alive," Bill said as he finished writing "It represents our level of understanding as of today. I'm sure in the following months we will uncover several other causes to add."

Terry Brand said she would run the diagram in the next issue of the *Press*. Bill said he would have a copy of the diagram enlarged and hung in his office. He added that he would provide amended copies as needed for committee meetings.

The cause-and-effect diagram had done exactly what Black had said it would, Bill thought to himself. It brought into focus relationships between otherwise unconnected actions. It would help each committee plan, and it had enhanced Bill's role as a knowledgeable leader and had reinforced the support he needed to make changes quickly.

As Bill brought the meeting to a close, he asked the manufacturers to prepare monthly summaries on their progress.

"We must share our progress as soon as we can to help everyone learn," he concluded.

In this meeting, Bill took the reins of leadership from Arthur Black. Bill made effective use of the flip chart and the cause-and-effect diagram. He identified that Black was instrumental in training him in effective use of the tools.

The meeting accomplished another vital task. Several of the local businesses will become the leaders in a variety of skills like design of experiments or work flow analysis. This provides valuable benchmarking as well as testing of the new skills.

Bill also provided the vision that there may be different skills, not just for different businesses, but for the different departments within one business. In a business, there frequently is a need to establish skills parochial to one department. For instance, problem solving in shipping and stores may have little in common with machining or memo typing.

51

Bill also laid the groundwork for a common process like a suggestion system and for simple problem solving using a common language for all. The selection of a common language will allow valuable ideas to be shared between functions. Thus, these ideas will more readily be accepted by management.

Midland City has progressed from awareness to measurement, to commitment, to plan, and to schedule. A similar sequence is needed for your organization. Also, Midland City has allowed for the varying needs of the different kinds of operations by providing training in different skills.

THE SUGGESTION SYSTEM

The announcement of a job managing the suggestion system and publicity for the process resulted in 37 applications. Bill and others from the city council interviewed every one of them. The slowdown of Midland City had created a labor pool of very high quality.

They chose Carol Kirk. She had been working in another town on the local newspaper for three years. She wanted to get closer to home. Carol had completed most of her degree in journalism when she and Joe Kirk married. They farmed just outside of town. Their two children were grown. Carol had computerized the farm records several years earlier. She had been active in the PTA and local politics and knew local people. Bill felt the fit was perfect. Carol had the skills, training, and experience.

Carol first went to Midland City Machine to learn its suggestion process. Next, she attended a workshop sponsored by the Employee Involvement Association (EIA) (previously the National Association of Suggestion Systems) on the effective ways of managing the suggestion process. At the workshop, Carol also found out about training, consulting, and commercially available software.

Midland City Machine already used special software that had the ability to associate each suggestion with strategic goals and processes. Carol doubted that a citywide process would need the sophistication that Midland City Machine required; but she could see the need for a PC-based software to track each suggestion with accuracy and efficiency.

Carol met with some of the workers in the different businesses. She found a new set of problems. Not all of the workers were convinced that there was a real commitment by management to share anything—anything of value that is.

Carol had another problem with the managers. They saw the suggestion process as a method to share wealth and power. Some managers did not want to share. Carol knew that she had her work cut out.

Carol needed help and a plan. Arthur Black was queried and he stated that suggestion systems were not one of his specialty areas. So Carol sought help from another consultant. She contacted Jake Paulson, a consultant with experience in actually running a suggestion system for a number of clients.

Jake Paulson pointed out that Carol's first step was to create a steering committee that represented all levels, from top management down, and people from each of the different kinds of businesses. The committee was limited to 20 persons and even that was viewed as too big to be efficient. Carol called a meeting of the committee to share a presentation from Jake Paulson and to develop guidelines for the suggestion process.

At the start of the meeting Carol explained that they all needed to better understand some of the possibilities that different kinds of suggestion systems could offer. This, she pointed out, was called benchmarking. Then Carol introduced Jake Paulson.

Jake provided a series of examples using videotapes, slides, and overhead transparencies. The roles of the typical suggestion system participants were discussed. These included suggesters, supervisors of suggesters, evaluators, management, and the suggestion system administrator.

The committee meeting ended with a fair amount of controversy. The teacher representative voiced concerns that suggestions could be contrary to negotiated rules. Some felt that their management would not allow any awards. Others felt that any awards to customers were not cost effective.

Carol brought in the mayor, Jake Paulson, and Arthur Black to settle these issues. Several meetings were necessary to get the committee and the organizations they represented to buy into the need for the process. After four weeks, Carol was able to call a second meeting of her committee.

Jake led the committee to identify what outputs the suggestion system must provide for everyone to do their jobs effectively. The committee charted what suggestion paperwork would flow into and out of each function. This input-output analysis of the desired suggestion system started at the beginning with designing the blank forms used by suggesters and ended with the recognition and awards.

The inputs and outputs were then defined. Details, such as the content of reports on the status of suggestions, the timeliness of answer suggestions, which departments were creating suggestions, and so on, were outlined. The reports' requirements identified the raw data needed from the input form, and the reports and inputs defined the software needed. There were a lot of differing needs, such as a small restaurant needing different outputs than a hospital.

Carol had her hands full in building a common approach support all organizations in Midland City.

There were some major direction items needed. What priority would be placed on team problem solving? Would peer-level team evaluations be utilized? Would the use of peer teams vary from one business to another? What level of awards would be paid to internal employees and to customers' suggestions? The steering committee found that it had to make a presentation to the mayor, the Manufacturing Committee, the Merchants Association, and the Chamber of Commerce to get the answers they needed to completely define the suggestion process.

Carol and her committee decided that they wanted to start by using a fairly simple form with limited data for the merchants, restaurants, and other service businesses. They also decided to recommend a more comprehensive process for the manufacturers. The ability to focus suggestion activity to support strategies in conformance with Baldrige criteria and tracking of process errors aimed at ISO 9000 would be vital.

The next task was for Carol to present the plan to the many merchants and business owners that were not represented on the steering committee. This turned into a tough sell.

Many of the smaller merchants were not too thrilled with the 1 percent sales tax and now faced the thought of Carol or anyone else saying "shame on you" when a customer turned in a gripe. Carol turned to Mayor Peterson to help sell the process. It was far from easy but finally a majority bought in and the rest accepted a wait-and-see posture.

The new process was ready for publication. The simple form for use with merchants and small businesses is shown on page 56. The more comprehensive form on page 58 is suitable for the larger organizations and allows the coding of the suggestions against strategies and processes among other features. This form would be evaluated within the company while the simpler forms would follow the sequence shown on page 57.

SMALL BUSINESS SUGGESTION SYSTEM FORM

	006160

QUALITY —
THE KEY TO OUR FUTURE
MIDLAND CITY SUGGESTION SYSTEM

Please fill out this form and place it in the locked box. The forms will be reviewed by the city Suggestion Administrator and then presented to the proper persons to correct the problem.

THANK YOU FOR HELPING MIDLAND CITY GROW

THE PROBLEM—Please describe the lack of quality or other problem.

It affects _____ Company

THE SOLUTION—Please state how quality could be improved or the problem corrected if you can (use reverse side if needed).

SUBMITTED BY: _____
Name   Phone No.

_____
Address

FOR SUGGESTION SYSTEM OFFICE USE

Idea Code _____
Repeat Idea _____
Merchant Notified _____ Suggester Thanked _____

In consideration of my participation in the Midland City Suggestion System, I agree that the use of this suggestion by Midland City or businesses therein shall not be the basis for a claim of any nature by me, my heirs, executors, or assigns.

CITYWIDE SUGGESTION SYSTEM SEQUENCE
FOR SMALL BUSINESS

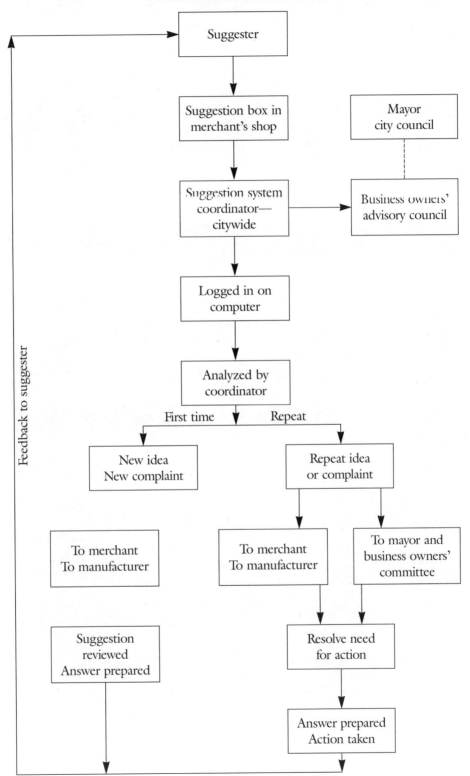

LARGE BUSINESS SUGGESTION SYSTEM FORM

Suggestion System

Supervisor Fill in
Last Digit of Year

Suggester Complete See Instructions & Eligibility Rules on Reverse Side of Suggester's Copy

☐ Individual ☐ Joint/Team ☐ Resubmit/Old Suggestion Number

Error, Problem, or Present Method:

Sort Field #1	Name
Sort Field #2	
Sort Field #3	

My Suggested Improvement (necessary to be eligible for cash awards):

Estimated Savings	$

My suggestion is submitted for consideration under the Terms/Rules of the Company Suggestion System as set forth on the reverse side of this form. I understand such Terms/Rules and agree that the Company, subsidiaries, and its successors and/or assignees shall have the absolute and exclusive right to my suggestion including patents.

**Suggester Eligible
for Cash Award
(Supervisor Complete)**

1st Suggester's Name (Print)

Last Name	First	Mi	Employee Soc. Sec. No.	Dept. No.	Building	Mail Station	Division	Suggester's Signature	☐ Yes ☐ No

2nd Suggester's Name (Print)

Last Name	First	Mi	Employee Soc. Sec. No.	Dept. No.	Building	Mail Station	Division	Suggester's Signature	☐ Yes ☐ No

More than 2 on team – attach list.

ACTION SEQUENCE

**Supervisors MUST complete SUGGESTION Number and Date Received at the time of SUBMISSION, prior to separation of the copies. This is the LEGAL DATE of the Suggestion.

1. **Supervisor of suggester**—Determine investigator and fill in line (2) or complete disposition if within your scope. Separate copies and send to appropriate areas.	Supervisor of Suggester (Print)	Mail Station	Dept. No.	Date Rec'd	Date Sent	Time Spent	Initial
2. **Area team evaluators**—Clarify and evaluate the suggestion. Reach agreement on potential savings with suggester enter dates recd. and sent, time spent, and send to expert evaluator.	Investigator's Name (Print)	Mail Station	Dept. No.	Date Rec'd	Date Sent	Time Spent	Initial
3. **Expert evaluator**—Verify evaluation and savings. Request funding and implement suggestion. Measure savings, evaluate award and review with team. Complete sign-off line and send to suggestion office.	Second Investigator's Name (Print)	Mail Station	Dept. No.	Date Rec'd	Date Sent	Time Spent	Initial
4. **Controller/industrial engineer**—Support funding and installation of suggestion. Verify potential and actual savings for award. Date and initial.	Industrial Engineer (Print)	Mail Station	Dept. No.	Date Rec'd	Date Sent	Time Spent	Initial
5. **Supervisor of suggester**—Review disposition and if approved, date, initial, and proceed to line (6). If not in agreement, work with investigator until agreement is worked out.	Supervisor of Suggester (Print)	Approval of Evaluation ☐ YES ☐ NO		Date Rec'd	Date Sent	Time Spent	Initial
6. **Suggester notified**—Complete and send action (white) copy to suggestion coordinator.	Suggester Notified ☐ YES ☐ NO	Suggester Is: ☐ On Leave	☐ Terminated ☐ Transferred	Suggester's Signature			Date
7. **Policy committee**—Reviews major awards and returns to system manager to process check, plan recognition, coodinator schedules reviews, requests checks, and sends check and copy of action copy to supervisor.	Subcommittee/Policy Committee			Date Rec'd	Date Sent		Date Complete

Investigator/Industrial Engineer Complete & Return to Suggester's Supervisor

Disposition (be specific):

FOR ADDITIONAL SPACE AND SAVINGS CALCULATIONS USE REVERSE SIDE OF THIS COPY

☐ Adopt	Date Installed	☐ Not Adopt	Date Not Adopted	NOTE:	Supervisors/Investigators: Keep the system updated on suggestion status. Submit update form when suggestion moves or investigator changes.

Suggestion Office Complete

Gross $ Saved	Cost to Implement	Net $ Saved	$ Awarded	Add on $	Date Completed	Award Type ☐ 1 ☐ 2 ☐ 3 ☐ 4

WHITE—ACTION COPY   YELLOW—SUGGESTION SYSTEM   PINK—DEPARTMENT COPY   GREEN—SUGGESTER COPY   SECOND WHITE—INVESTIGATOR'S REPORT COPY

LARGE BUSINESS SUGGESTION SYSTEM SEQUENCE

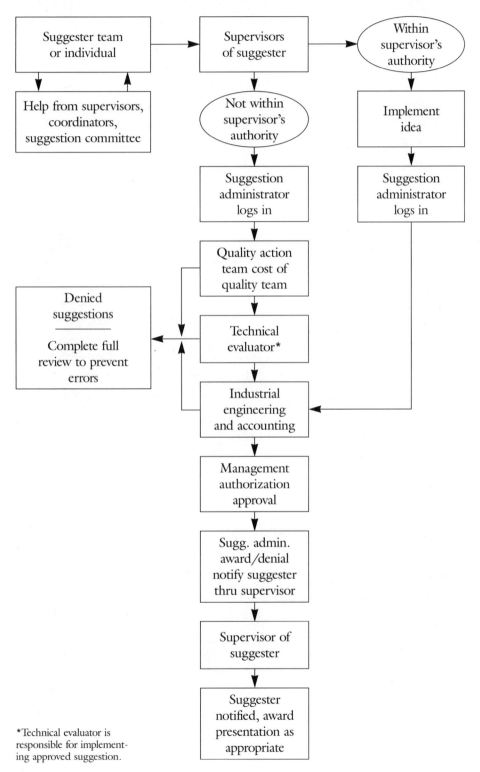

*Technical evaluator is responsible for implementing approved suggestion.

Quickly answering suggestions was one requirement that was drilled at the EIA workshop and by Jake Paulson. The citywide system for the small businesses would aim to completely process a suggestion within two weeks. Particularly with customers involved, the timeliness became crucial. A similar aim for internal systems was established.

The approved suggestion process incorporated the following:

1. An award of 10 percent of the first year's savings that the suggestion generated was established. Businesses could pay in cash or in merchandise as they chose.

2. Teams for all larger organizations would be encouraged by increasing the award's percentage by the number of persons on the team.

3. Evaluations of customer suggestions for local merchants would follow the sequence shown on page 57. Evaluations of the suggestions from internal employees of larger businesses (see page 59) would be made first by the supervisor, since most suggestions would be within his or her authority to implement. If the supervisor could not implement the suggestion or chose to deny it, the idea would go to the suggestion administrator and be assigned to a peer evaluation team. The team would clarify and, if possible, enhance the concept of the idea and send it to a final evaluation by the technical or administrative person responsible for the process. Completed evaluations would be processed either by Carol or the internal administrator at the company.

4. Carol was convinced that publicity and promotion of the suggestion process was vital. She persuaded the Merchants Association to provide color televisions as prizes awarded during quarterly drawings made from suggestions that had generated tangible or measurable savings.

5. All suggestions returned to their author would carry a drawing ticket stub. It showed the suggesters were included in the drawing or it provided an explanation of why their idea did not generate tangible savings.

After the program started, there were the predictable problems. Some of the evaluations took far longer than necessary and the Merchants Association had to do some persuading. Collecting the suggestions also had some failures, and two merchants' suggestion boxes went two months without a collection. Some merchants did not keep the rack of forms and a box that were provided by the Merchants Association in a visible and convenient place.

The first few months gradually found increasing participation and merchants started posting the best suggestion of the week in their windows. Folks reading these suggestions got ideas of their own. The display of the television sets also spurred participation. Every merchant that displayed the TVs had more suggestions while the TVs were in the window.

Also, only the merchants that supported the suggestion process could have the TVs to display and could be listed on the brochure explaining the process and the merchants' dedication to customer satisfaction. The chance of winning a TV as a prize led many customers to shop the merchants in the program.

Carol next persuaded the *Midland City Press* to feature the weekly winning suggestions, the evaluators that had the fastest turnaround, and the businesses that had the highest levels of participation. Also, customers from out of town that won awards were featured in their hometown papers leading to greater publicity for Midland City.

As the process matured, the need for summary reports to management, or in some cases to the Merchants Association, became obvious. Carol used some of Midland City Machine's reports. One liked by all was a summary report featuring the total costs of the process compared to the savings. This was dubbed the "bottom line" report and it is shown on page 62.

After a year of operation, the continuous maturing of the suggestion process caused increasing contributions of 10 percent of the savings to the city fund and led to a gradual elimination of the 1 percent sales tax.

Carol was asked to make a presentation at the regional EIA conference since the success of a suggestions system for a community was unusual. In her presentation, Carol pointed out that every large business was, in a way, a community made up of functions with little in common like shipping, manufacturing, and sales. Her conclusion after months of operation was that a successful suggestion system requires careful planning to generate ownership, supported by the top management of all functions involved.

As the suggestion system was used, Carol found that most merchants believe that their customers were truly impressed with Midland City's plans. The customers felt they had become part of the businesses they patronized. The merchants were competing with stores in nearby towns so any advantage they could gain was definitely worthwhile. And they liked gaining something tangible for the 1 percent of sales they were assessed.

The more enthusiastic merchants posted the best suggestions along with the names of the authors in their windows. Some held their own drawings and gave out gift certificates redeemable at their stores.

Of course, there were nonbelievers. Some said they were happy with the way things were and didn't need Carol Kirk or anyone else telling

SUGGESTION SYSTEM MONTHLY STATUS REPORT

Report Date: 11/15/92   November Report

	1992 Nov.	1991 Nov.	YTD
Number awarded	3	0	6
Number not adopted	1	0	1
Total completed	7	0	10
Number received total	13	0	19
Number remaining open	8	0	9
Total savings	219,300.00	0.00	285,978.00
Total answer cost	0.00		0.00
Total awards	10,250.00		10,358.00
Total implementation cost	18,780.00		19,030.00
Total costs	29,030.00	0.00	29,388.00
Bottom line $	190,270.00	0.00	256,590.00

Closed Suggestions:

Nov 1992	Total	% Total	Resubmits	% Total	$ Saved	Hrs. Spent	$/Hour	Ans. Cost
Tangible	7	100.00	0	0.00	219,300	14.80	0.00	0.00
Intangible	0	0.00	0	0.00	0	0.00	0.00	0.00
Safety	0	0.00	0	0.00	0	0.00	0.00	0.00
Miscellaneous	0	0.00	0	0.00	0	0.00	0.00	0.00
Total (Nov)	7	100.00	0	0.00	219,300	14.80	0.00	0.00

Year to Date

	Total	% Total	Resubmits	% Total	$ Saved	Hrs. Spent	$/Hour	Ans. Cost
Tangible	10	100.00	0	0.00	285,978	15.80	0.00	0.00
Intangible	0	0.00	0	0.00	0	0.00	0.00	0.00
Safety	0	0.00	0	0.00	0	0.00	0.00	0.00
Miscellaneous	0	0.00	0	0.00	0	0.00	0.00	0.00
Total (YTD)	10	100.00	0	0.00	285,978	15.80	0.00	0.00

Open Suggestions:

Age of suggestion	0–30 Days	31–60 Days	61–90 Days	Over 90 Days
Total	9	1	0	0
Total estimated savings	$16,066.00	$22,000.00	$0.00	$0.00

NOTE: Total cost includes answer costs, implementation costs, and awards to suggesters. Year-to-date figures are for the current fiscal year (01/01/92). Total savings figures apply to any suggestion with dollar savings (regardless of the type of suggestion). Cost breakdowns are not available for Nov. 1991.

them how to run their businesses. Carol personally visited those merchants to tell them how the other businesses had profited from the system.

Some merchants participated but were hesitant to make the suggested improvements. At the city council's recommendation, the Midland City Merchants Association established a task team to determine how to convince those merchants to improve their services or products. The team included both believers and nonbelievers.

After several meetings the team members concluded that they all could gain financially by participating in the system. They decided that everyone had to participate if Midland City was to have a quality image. But they needed some teeth in their enforcement.

After they announced their findings, some nonbelievers remained just that; however, about 25 percent of those who originally had rejected the idea agreed they had been foolish in not responding to the suggestion system.

To further enhance participation, only those merchants who supported the system were given banners proclaiming their support. The real pressure came from the Midland City Merchants Association and their families, friends, employees, and customers, or their lack of customers as their businesses declined. Midland City residents began to back the system, and merchants who didn't became increasingly unpopular.

The pressure on the merchants wasn't organized but it was effective. Local people saw the access to the suggestion system as a potential reward if they found money-saving ideas. There was a shift toward doing business with merchants that were part of the process. A few saw the benefits to Midland City being unified. After only 10 months of operation, Carol found she had nearly all of the merchants participating. Carol gave a lot of credit to Terry Brand for the publicity on winners and merchants.

As months passed, the benefits of the system became more evident. Reports of dollars saved spurred additional interest, especially from the *Midland City Press*.

Carol Kirk was convinced that the suggestion system was a major key to quality for Midland City. Besides, it made the process of change fun and profitable for customers, employees, and businesses.

Establishing a suggestion system on a citywide basis is difficult when it incorporates both businesses and city employees. The process can be done. It is necessary that the needs of several levels of participants be met. Carol made sure of that by using her EIA training and consultant Jake Paulson to benchmark the process and to lead her committee to defining the required data inputs and outputs. Carol made use of proven processes from other organizations tailored to the needs of her community.

In your organization you face many of the same needs. There will be departments with widely differing cultures and work styles. You need to provide the executive and steering committees with enough knowledge to select the features of a process that best meet your needs. There is no such thing as a canned suggestion process. The needs of each organization differ enough that it is sound business practice to carefully tailor your suggestion system.

Midland City Machine had found that its suggestion software can become a repository for all quality improvement ideas whether from an individual, a group, an assigned quality improvement team, technical staff, or management.

Once you capture all quality improvements in your software, you can create reports showing processes and procedures causing errors, departments with high error rates, evaluators with fast turnaround times, and other indicators of quality. This data become vital to total quality management.

The ability to tie suggestions or improvements to published strategies will reinforce pursuit of a Baldrige Award. Also, the ability to better identify error-prone processes by your quality improvements could be vital in the future for ISO 9000 certification.

TRAINING

Setting up an adult training program in statistical process control and team problem solving was beyond the normal demands of Superintendent Helen Sikorski and her staff. She anticipated morale problems if she tried to force her teachers into the new tasks. But she was determined to find a way.

She hired instructors from the nearby technical institute to train her volunteers who, in turn, would train everyone else. Fortunately, more than enough teachers and recently retired teachers, engineers, and managers from Midland City manufacturers volunteered to be trainers.

They began the two-month training course that fall. Meanwhile, Bill helped Helen form a steering committee of manufacturers, merchants, and school district administrators. The committee's job was to determine the level of training needed at each business and to schedule training sessions.

Helen knew what a massive task it would be to educate all of Midland City's workers. She would have to change her own management style. From what she had read about education in Japan, she was convinced that, ultimately, she would have to retrain her classroom teachers to use statistics in their classrooms in the earliest grades possible. But first her teachers had to learn how to use statistics and accept the need for a curriculum change.

She also knew that teachers were a key element in community acceptance. They were role models and their acceptance was vital.

The steering committee decided what category of workers to train in what order after the trainers finished their courses.

First, teachers and school administrators would finish 20 hours of training in team problem solving and 20 more hours in statistical process control (SPC) in five months. Math and shop teachers, however, would have 56 hours in SPC to allow for more complete training in their subject areas.

Next, managers, supervisors, technicians, and assigned facilitators at all Midland City manufacturing plants would go through 20 hours of team problem solving training and 56 hours of statistics. They would finish three months after the school employees and would establish a joint process coordinating committee so all companies could share what they learned.

Next, factory and office workers at Midland City manufacturing plants would have 20 hours of training in team problem solving and eight hours in SPC. They would complete their training four months after their managers.

Helen had been concerned about training factory workers. Many of them, she thought, would find 56 hours of training threatening. She knew they could learn the material, but some had never gone to college or even graduated from high school and were uncomfortable in an academic setting. In addition, the team problem solving training emphasized conference leadership, team building, and decision making normally not a part of a factory worker's daily life.

As usual, Arthur Black came to the rescue. He suggested, and Helen agreed, that the factory workers complete the entire team problem solving course, but that their SPC training be stretched over a longer period of time with much of it done through actual work situations.

After the factory and office workers, Midland City merchants, city managers, and supervisors would have 20 hours in team problem solving and 56 hours in SPC. They would finish four months after the factory workers. Then the merchants' employees would go through 20 hours in team problem solving training and 56 hours in SPC. Their training in SPC would also be stretched over a longer period of time. They would finish four months after their bosses completed their training. The entire cycle would take 20 months. It was a long, massive training program, but with the hundreds of people involved, Helen felt fortunate it would take only that amount of time.

After a month of training, the trainers briefed Helen and her steering committee on what they had learned. They touched briefly on basic SPC techniques, including Pareto charts and cause-and-effect diagrams, and they reviewed Deming's 14 management principles. They stressed the need for using statistical controls during production to ensure that a product is good before it makes it to the inspection stage. They also reviewed how SPC techniques were usable in retail stores, banks, and hospitals. Helen's employees showed how SPC could help teach and administer in the schools.

As the trainers continued their report, one steering committee member suggested that Midland City could easily guarantee quality by carefully inspecting each product before shipment. One trainer, immediately challenging that argument, asked all the committee members if they thought they could inspect a part they knew as well as their employers. Almost everyone answered "yes."

"Do I have a test for you!" the trainer responded as she displayed a test paragraph on the overhead projector, written by Noriniko Nakayama, president of Fiji Tsu American.

> *You see, quality control is not just a little room adjacent to the factory floor, whose occupants make a nuisance of themselves to everyone else. Quality control is, or should be, a state of mind. It permeates the entire operation. Everyone, from president to the production trainee, is part of quality control. But it is up to top management to instill in everyone the desire to produce goods of the highest quality.*

She gave them one minute to count the number of times the letter *E* appeared in the paragraph. No one could agree on a number. "Even proofreaders rarely can," the trainer said. She had effectively made her point regarding the difficulty an inspection department has in weeding out a bad product from a given batch.

"The obvious answer is to create a system that is as error-free as possible and reduce the need for inspections," she said.

The SPC course, the trainers said, was organized into a number of sections covering the following material:

- An overview of the international nature of business competition and the resulting conclusion that the United States must either achieve quality production or, in effect, become a second-class nation

- A review of the impact of Sarasohn, Juran, and Deming on Japan and an understanding of how their principles should be woven into the manufacturing culture

- The use of improvement teams to analyze problems and determine solutions

- Effective project selection using brainstorming, prioritization, and analysis

- How to collect data using flow charts and cause-and-effect diagrams and how to construct a Pareto chart from the data

- The measurement of median, central location, shape, and variability of data

- The development of histograms, distribution curves, and an understanding of the measure of variance

- The application of data techniques to process control and the use of $\bar{X}$ and R charts and familiarity with other chart formats

- The analysis of process capability using both arithmetic and chart techniques

- The use of median and individual charts for process control

- The use of attribute charts for process control

Helen was amazed at the depth of the problem-solving techniques involved. She hadn't used statistics since she studied for her doctorate. But, for Midland City, the focus would be limited to a relatively simplified process with direct application. With the proper amount of management support, the knowledge of SPC would make a difference in the quality of work.

The trainers had viewed videotapes that explained the culture of team problem solving for teams or quality circles and how people must learn to work as a team and to handle the hostility that often accompanies working in groups.

Team training includes team building, use of nominal group technique, and an understanding of decision-making processes that the team could seek help on if appropriate. Basic SPC skills were to be a part of the team training since the ability to gather data was needed if the solutions to problems were to be found. Nominal group technique (NGT) was presented as a structured form of brainstorming with a voting process to lead the team to a conclusion. The NGT process coupled with seeking data on what was really happening provided the basis for solutions to tough business problems.

Team members are formed around natural work units where they share common knowledge or common concerns. The team members have the knowledge of how things really work and with training and skills can help change the process or procedure involved. The trainers stressed that 80 percent of the problems are caused by the processes and procedures and only 20 percent by employees. With teams, employees feel they have the power to change the system to improve their work quality.

The same trainer suggested that each team adopt a name to give the group members a sense of identity.

"Circles or teams bring about a feeling of old-fashioned team spirit, especially because participation is voluntary. And the solutions they offer through group consensus are far more creative than individual solutions," he said.

"Team participants first need to know what is expected of them in order to achieve anything," another trainer advised. "Then they must determine how they will measure their productivity. The measures should reflect their output in relation to their input and should be specific, but easy to understand. The measures should be selected by the team, such as number of bad parts produced or number of invoices retyped. The team should collect its own data to measure change. The team needs to be in control of its project."

"After teams have successfully solved some problems, they are more able to set reasonable goals for improvement," a third trainer said. "But they need regular feedback for their members and management on how they are progressing toward their goals."

"Each team or circle must elect a leader and be provided with a facilitator—a person from outside the group who will help guide the problem solving process," added the fourth trainer. "They also need to be supported by a steering committee that includes top managers, to establish policies, objectives, and management support.

"Communication between employees and management is essential for successful teams."

After the meeting, Helen listened to one of Deming's tapes. "It's all so simple—so simple," Deming's recorded voice calmly stated.

The concepts may be simple, Helen thought, but she and the other leaders in the quality program would have to work hard to convince everyone to use them.

It was going to be an interesting process, she said to herself as she switched off the tape recorder.

My studies show that change in behaviors will result from four causes.

Rewards—*There is a proven history of behavior tied to reward and recognition. Rewards can only motivate people to accomplish results within their skills or capabilities.*

Training—*Providing training is a form of empowerment. Management affirms the value of the employees and their ideas through training. Training, coupled with rewards and reinforcement of the new skills, is powerful.*

Culture—*The change of culture to one that values people and drives fear out of the organization will encourage pride in the work and participation in the correction of processes and prevention of errors. Culture alone will not lead to the total quality organization.*

Hawthorne effect—*These studies from the 1920s show that almost anything management does for employees will have a positive, if short-term, effect. The message here is that if you start anything, you will see results in the short term. It is vital to have long-term data to affirm the value of any change in culture, rewards, or training.*

MIDLAND CITY SCHOOLS

The Midland City school district was a consolidated district that had incorporated the schools from its surrounding smaller communities in the early 1970s. As superintendent, Helen Sikorski had gained immense respect for her work in uniting the schools both physically and spiritually.

Her new task, however, seemed even more complex. She had accepted the challenge of training all interested adults in SPC and team problem solving or quality circles, and integrating those processes, in one form or another, into Midland City schools. She was also determined to increase the students' SAT scores significantly.

The day after Arthur Black's speech at the council meeting, Helen met with council member Susan Anderson, a high school civics teacher. They reviewed their objectives and formed a steering committee with Joel Larson, the high school librarian, and John Schmidt, the junior high school industrial arts department head.

Their task was extraordinarily difficult. They had to learn new techniques and apply them to a school environment, and become training resources for the entire community.

As teachers, they had learned basic statistics in college, but they had never even heard of the sophisticated processes businesses use to increase productivity and quality. They all agreed that learning and then teaching statistical process control indeed would be a challenge.

Another challenge would be to bring the teachers' union into the change process. Some teachers would resent change and urge their union representatives to lobby for the status quo. Helen knew she would have to carefully recruit creative and aggressive teachers to help plan and implement the training.

They appointed four subcommittees to focus on specific training areas.

1. Adult education in SPC and team problem solving

2. Elementary and secondary school curriculum changes to include basic statistics and team exercises

3. The use of team problem solving or quality circles and SPC by school administrators

4. The improvement of SAT scores

ADULT EDUCATION

At the strategic planning meeting, Mayor Bill Peterson had established an optimistic schedule to train all working adults. He knew that once the adults were trained, changes in elementary and secondary education would happen more easily.

The classes for the volunteer trainers were held during evenings at Midland City High School. The classroom lights burned until 9:00 most nights as trainees reviewed the material on team problem solving and SPC. The lights were one indication of action; another indication was the conversation during coffee breaks and at local restaurants. People were using words like *variance* in their casual discussions about sports.

The volunteer trainers were divided into two groups. Although both groups were trained in both subjects, one group concentrated on teams or quality circles and the other on SPC.

When they finished their training, they began training other Midland City adults. Bill, himself, trained extensively in both areas. He was impressed by everybody's enthusiasm.

Town meetings were held twice a month at City Hall with well-known speakers on economic planning and local reports and panel discussions. The meetings always finished with cookies, cake, or pie, and good conversation. Free child care services were provided in the lounge so all parents could attend.

After a year of training, the adult education committee members began looking at including training in value analysis and work flow analysis, even though they had much work left in teams or quality circles and statistics. They knew they had to keep moving ahead.

ELEMENTARY AND SECONDARY SCHOOL CURRICULUM CHANGES

As expected, attempting to change the curriculum in Midland City schools was a hotly debated topic. Some teachers, parents, and students saw change as threatening. Helen Sikorski did her best to assure them that the additional training would not replace previously approved classroom instruction.

Still, some teachers felt they already had too much to do and saw the additional material as a burden. Many wanted to use the same lesson plans and teaching aids they had used for years. Change was risky and a waste of time, they argued.

As a former teacher Helen understood their concerns, but she was convinced that Midland City students were not entering their careers as well positioned for success as they could be.

The curriculum subcommittee was comprised of five teachers, an industry representative, and a professor of business from Meadan University, with Arthur Black as an adviser. It was responsible for recommending how the district could upgrade the curriculum. It met with officials from a school district in another state that had successfully taught quality circle techniques and statistics to its students. It also met with industry leaders, who reinforced its belief that students who learned the processes would have an advantage when looking for jobs. Terry Brand carried reports of these meetings in the *Midland City Press*.

The committee members found themselves in the role of innovators. Team problem solving, for the most part, was foreign to Midland City schools. Statistics were not a part of the district's traditional training and were rarely used in classroom lectures. Thus, there were few teaching examples available.

A week before school started the following year, the teachers attended a workshop designed to show them how Pareto diagrams—a process for presenting relative order of importance, histograms, and cause-and-effect diagrams—could be used in the classroom.

"A history teacher, for example, could use Pareto charting to show the magnitude of impact world wars or major disease epidemics have on the economy," explained Helen Sikorski during the workshop.

The processes could be used in varying degrees of sophistication at every grade level, she said.

"The objective is to make statistical comparison a basic tool for better understanding in a variety of subject areas. Your students must learn a respect for data and the skills to accumulate the needed data for effective decision making," Helen concluded.

Math teachers were the first group to adjust their curriculum to include basic statistical techniques. Helen worked gradually to change the minds of the teachers who called the training a waste of time by having those teachers willing to change serve as leaders in the circles and planning teams. Faculty meetings featured how various teachers worked the new methods into their classroom materials. Eventually, recognition for accomplishment coupled with strong persuasion caused most teachers to comply.

Using team problem solving for classroom projects helped to resolve a number of communication problems typical of teenagers, as Helen predicted. The process forced a variety of students to work together—students who normally would not have. Working in teams helped the students build their self-images.

Several students worked in teams to research projects. They used statistics to prepare their reports and to provide logical presentations of facts.

There were problems due to untrained team leaders and participants, but the new teaching methods did enhance student learning. One of the team processes, *nominal group technique,* became a byword for resolving conflicting opinions. NGT became a frequent phrase.

By spring, the students began to expect better quality reports from their classmates and complained when the reports failed to meet their expectations.

Helen noticed that students were beginning to think more logically. The industry representative involved was delighted as he thought of employees having those skills. It was a tough first year, but Helen felt her district would soon be a model for other districts to follow.

THE USE OF TEAM PROBLEM SOLVING AND SPC BY SCHOOL ADMINISTRATORS

The subcommittee members in charge of integrating quality circles into the schools found a number of good models to study. Many schools, they determined, successfully use circles in the following ways:

• Administrators and teachers use them to determine school policies.

- Students use them to influence decisions on course content and teacher performance.
- Teachers and board members use them to negotiate salary contracts and policy issues.
- Custodians use them to solve maintenance problems.
- Students and teachers use them to determine discipline policies.

The subcommittee members organized four teams: one with administrators, a second with teachers, a third with custodians, and a fourth with students. The circle members were charged with suggesting how to improve their schools and to attack critical problems.

By the end of the first year, the four teams were operating with mixed success. The student team had suggested several changes—some realistic, some not.

Most of their early suggestions were actually complaints about restrictions, water fountains, rest rooms, cafeteria food, and special fees. As the team matured, however, it addressed deeper concerns such as how to discipline disruptive students.

The custodian team hadn't really moved beyond complaining about disruptive students, smoking in the rest rooms, and the need for updated equipment. Helen felt the facilitator was not properly guiding that group.

The administration team looked for ways to streamline recordkeeping and audiovisual maintenance efforts. The members created a subteam of office clerical workers who performed a wide range of duties including typing assignments and posting student data for teachers. The workers, who felt they were overloaded with work, fully agreed with Vilfredo Pareto's 80-20 rule: They were convinced that 20 percent of the teachers caused 80 percent of their problems.

The clerical team members listed their most common complaints of teachers. Some constantly requested that material be retyped because of last-minute changes; many teachers gave typists illegible or incomplete drafts; and many teachers turned in their drafts late.

The clerical workers wanted to find a way to minimize the need for retyping drafts, which led to extra work and overtime. They started by logging all the typing they did daily, noting the times they had to retype drafts and rush orders that demanded overtime. They collected data for three months and determined that of the 93 teachers, only 24 teachers used the typing service during that time. Using a Pareto process they prioritized the 24 teachers according to the number of times they asked for revisions. The chart showed the ratio of page revisions required divided by the pages of new typing submitted.

CLERICAL WORK DATA

Teacher	Original Typing Pages	Revised Pages of Typing	Number of Pages Submitted Late Requiring Overtime
1	6	17	
2	10	5	
3	7	15	7
4	10	2	
5	6	3	
6	3		
7	10		
8	2		
9	10	2	5
10	10	15	
11	3		
12	12	2	12
13	2		
14	4		
15	8	2	
16	17	1	
17	11	18	11
18	2		
19	10	1	
20	10	2	
21	10	6	
22	12	12	
23	10	14	
24	8		

Of the 24 teachers, 16 requested revisions. Only six of the teachers had revision counts equal to new pages they submitted for typing. Helen was faced with a tough problem. The teachers identified as the sources for excessive revisions were some of her best. She didn't want them to become defensive, yet she couldn't ignore the circle's findings.

Helen and the team members arranged a meeting with the 16 teachers. After the team members presented their findings, she added her concerns about the costs of interfering with excellent teachers and asked the teachers and the team members to brainstorm for possible solutions.

Language arts teacher Tammy Lord suggested that the district invest in modern word processing equipment and scrap its obsolete typewriters.

RATIO OF REVISIONS TO NEW TYPING

$$\text{RATIO} = \frac{\text{REVISIONS REQUIRED}}{\text{NEW TYPING}}$$

Teacher	Ratio
1	2.83
2	.5
3	2.14
4	.2
5	.5
6	0
7	0
8	0
9	.2
10	1.5
11	0
12	.16
13	0
14	0
15	.25
16	.05
17	1.64
18	0
19	0.1
20	.2
21	.6
22	1.0
23	1.4
24	0

Elementary school teacher James Riley recommended that all teachers attend a workshop on effective planning and writing.

"If you're going to discourage corrections, students will end up with error-filled tests and handouts," warned science teacher Bill Simond.

"Whatever we do," Helen assured, "we have to support the staff with positive suggestions and not sabotage it with negative criticism."

Helen divided them into two teams of six. She explained that two teams working independently would bring about the best solutions and also would build togetherness and ownership of the solutions.

After two months, the teams agreed on a recommendation. The district, they decided, should purchase a word processing system with

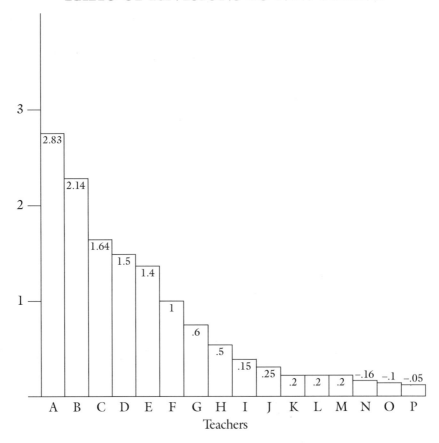

RATIO OF REVISIONS TO NEW TYPING

several online terminals. Teachers as well as the typists could use the terminals to submit, correct, and update drafts. The school board members agreed to the purchase.

A second survey was taken three months after the new equipment was installed. The total number of corrections and changes had almost doubled, an indication that more teachers were more frequently revising their materials. Under the old system, some teachers avoided revising their work because the secretaries were always extremely busy. With the new system, the teachers themselves could readily insert corrections. The result was better quality tests and handouts. Bill Simond was pleased that his concern was not neglected.

The clerical workers' labor was down by 15 percent, and overtime had been almost eliminated. Teachers spent less time making minor corrections on word processors than they did previously by carefully marking copy.

The faculty team was quite successful in applying the process to salary negotiations. The teachers applied statistical concepts to the packages they and the district representatives proposed. Working as a team they found they could separate emotional issues from economic issues. They were able to present their recommendations to their colleagues logically and statistically.

THE INCREASE OF SAT SCORES

Helen's call for academic excellence brought her face-to-face with some basic issues.

- The curriculum would have to be strengthened to focus on overall excellence rather than on competence achievement. Students who failed a grade would have to repeat that grade.

- Parents would have to become more involved in and supportive of their children's learning. As a result, their children would have less time for chores and jobs.

- A strict discipline policy would have to be followed to prevent disruptive students from interfering with the learning process.

- And, perhaps the most controversial, the students would have to achieve a C average or better to participate in extracurricular activities. Helen hoped she wouldn't have to bench a star quarterback for a bad grade.

Helen knew that she needed to change both the attitudes and practice of teachers, parents, and the entire community. On the surface, such change seemed simple, but in reality, it required a massive change of behaviors.

Designing a discipline policy was tougher than she had expected. Since discipline was a major problem and an extremely emotional issue, Helen decided to use a team of selectively recruited parents, teachers, and principals.

The parents represented the entire gamut, from those who actively supported education to those who didn't. Likewise, the range of teachers included those who rarely had discipline problems to those continually plagued by troublesome students. The team included a junior high and a senior high principal.

Terry Brand gave the discipline team extensive publicity in the *Press*. The more important the circle members were made to feel, the more likely they were to really address the problem, both Helen and Terry rationalized.

At their first meeting, the members agreed that improving SAT scores would enhance the image of their town and would help draw new businesses to Midland City. They believed that disruptive students posed a threat to effective learning because the students often took too much of a teacher's valuable time.

English teacher Dina Harold presented data showing that disruptive students were more likely to come from homes where parents provided little support for their education.

"We need to get after these parents," said Carol Williams, a social studies teacher.

"But troublesome students don't always come from uncaring or unconcerned parents," said science teacher Matt Williams. "Some of these kids are being raised by single parents who don't have enough time to spend with their kids because they're working all the time just to stay ahead."

The adult group, unable to reach a conclusion, decided that students should tackle the problem. After all, the majority of the students resented troublemakers and show-offs for interfering with their education.

A student team was formed and included both model students and those who had discipline problems. The team met with the parent-teacher circle three times to share its view of the problems.

The students traveled to Meadan twice to visit schools with model discipline policies. Each trip was publicized in the school paper and a story was published in the *Press*. After four months they proposed a new set of rules which was approved by 90 percent of the student body. Among other things, the rules prohibited disruptive behavior because it interfered with the desires of the majority. They identified vandalism as unacceptable and punishable by suspension and legal action.

Six months after the SAT committee members first met, they arranged several study sessions for students who planned to take SAT and other standardized tests. They selectively chose samples of test scores from previous years to measure improvement.

The committee members agreed with the teachers that test scores are only one indication of a student's ability. They realized that some students simply are better test takers than others, so other measurements were used too.

The *Press* regularly featured pictures of honor roll and National Honor Society students, and students who were in especially effective study or circle groups. It didn't take long for students to begin competing for the publicity, thus improving their performance. Academic achievement had never before been viewed with such importance.

After one year, Helen was convinced that Midland City was on the right track. SAT scores had yet to improve significantly, but she was confident that they would. She wasn't expecting a quick fix; she was working for change that would last a long time.

A year before, she gladly would have left Midland City for the super-intendency offer she received a week before. But after witnessing Midland City schools' progress, she knew she could not give up what she considered to be one of the most exciting jobs in the state.

Superintendent Helen Sikorski is obviously both a visionary to plan the job and a supreme politician to gain the participation of all parties. She used committees on the four training areas to both specify process and gain ownership. She also created a path for gaining the publicity vital to promoting the new behaviors. The keys to this process are ownership in the definition of the approach, Helen's leadership, and outreach to the whole community.

SCOTT'S PROJECT

Scott barged into the living room where his father was reading the evening paper. He was frustrated.

"Dad, I think you've got me into the final mess of this productivity thing," he said as he threw himself on the couch. "Our teacher has assigned us to teams of five, and each team has to find a new way to use the concepts of statistical process control, quality circles, team problem solving, or overall quality improvement methods.

"On top of that," Scott continued, "she said our grades will be 'significantly impacted' by how well we do on our projects!"

Scott was fuming. His 10th grade social studies teacher said that the projects would teach the students how to do independent research in teams as well as teach them about quality processes. They would have to come up with new ideas, the teacher said, and therefore, they would not be able to use the library and plagiarize someone else's work.

"I won't be able to come up with anything worthwhile," Scott complained.

It didn't take Bill long to realize that Scott was trying to get him to do the homework assignment. Bill knew he had to help Scott, but he also knew that Scott would never learn how to be an independent researcher and creative thinker if Dad always did all of the work for him. Bill discussed the assignment with Scott but specifically tried not to tell Scott what to do.

"You'll have to find a problem with variables that you can measure and use team problem-solving techniques to bring about the best ideas on how to solve the problem," Bill told his son.

The next day after school Scott met with his four teammates at Tom's Cafe. "My father wasn't much help," he reported. His teammates were disappointed. They had hoped that the mayor of Midland City and the leader of its quest for quality would become their source of inspiration and knowledge, and save them a lot of work. Two of the teammates had likewise accosted their parents for quick solutions and had come up with relatively empty bags.

After some discussion they decided to apply some of the nominal group techniques they had learned as the methodology to determine the basis of their project.

As the first step, they each took a piece of paper and, with Scott's leadership, used a technique known in NGT as *silent generation*. It calls for each person to spend about 10 minutes listing all solutions that he or she can think of to solve a problem.

After the 10 minutes, they combined their lists of ideas for the project using a round-robin method for gathering plus consolidation.

- Improve the performance of the Cougar hockey players.
- Improve the food quality in the cafeteria.
- Improve the quality of auto repairs in the different garages in town.
- Improve the quality of coaches at school.
- Reduce the amount of food waste in the school cafeteria.
- Improve the quality of textbooks in school.

Next, the students discussed each item and rated the measures or data available and the relative importance and contribution each of the quality improvement ideas would have on Midland City. They eventually voted to study how to reduce the food waste in the high school cafeteria.

High school students were served a standard hot lunch, with no variance in the size of the servings. The problem was many of the students, especially the girls, were regularly dieting and threw away much of their food. Also, different students liked different foods. Students who didn't like their food often swapped with other students, but there was still a lot of food thrown away.

Scott and his teammates knew something could be done at the serving line to reduce food waste. But before they determined what, they had to collect data on the number and type of students who ate hot lunches.

During the next two weeks they kept track of the age, sex, and eating habits of each student who ate hot lunches, keeping track of the varying waste day to day and item to item. Measuring garbage, they quickly realized, was a yucky job.

At their next meeting they compiled the data and found a definite correlation between students who threw away large amounts of food and students who sought more nourishment every day. Again, they used nominal group techniques to identify potential solutions, to vote on those solutions, to identify the risks of the potential solutions, and to vote on them again.

They decided that food waste could be reduced by offering students five hot lunch options that ranged from half orders to extra portions of everything. To monitor the students' choices, they suggested that a marker system be used. Marker cards would indicate the portion of food a student wanted. Each student would pick up one at the start of the serving line and show the card to the food servers as the student moved down the line with his or her tray. The students would turn in the markers along with their payment to the cashier. The team members also suggested that the payments be adjusted so that students would pay according to what they ordered.

Scott realized he had learned a valuable lesson. By using a sequential application of nominal group technique and touching on decision analysis, he and his teammates understood that a simple control of quantity and/or eliminating certain items were not only desirable but almost necessary to reduce food waste.

Soon after the team members finished their report, they presented it to their classmates and teacher. Some students questioned whether the school would even consider such a change because it would call for at least five different prices. Scott and his team members were confident that if public cafeterias could deal with infinite variables, the school cafeteria could deal with five.

After the other six teams presented their reports, the class voted to suggest the cafeteria changes to Helen Sikorski and the cafeteria staff, who eventually agreed to try it for three months.

Fortunately, Scott's team had collected several weeks of data on the exact poundage of waste in the cafeteria. The data provided Sikorski with a base from which she could compare any changes in the level of waste during the trial three months.

For the first few days, the cafeteria was mass confusion even though the new serving system was heavily advertised in the school newspaper and over the loudspeaker. Students who were not used to making decisions were suddenly forced to determine whether they wanted lunch one, two, three, four, or five. Screaming complaints were heard when students found out they had selected extra mashed potatoes and gravy when they actually wanted half portions.

After the first week, however, the changes began to settle in. The students liked having options, and the food servers heard fewer complaints. Food waste dropped to less than a third of what it had been before the new system. The only party that felt a loss was Torkelson's Hog Farm, which relied on the school cafeteria waste for hog food.

Bill was proud of Scott. He had hoped Scott would find some way to contribute to Midland City's pursuit of quality. The class assignment was an excellent way to have high school students use and understand statistical data gathering and application, he told Scott's classroom teacher.

"I'm thankful also because you gave Scott the chance to earn extra credit," Bill told the teacher. "He definitely needs to improve his grades."

This is an example of a fairly new problem-solving team. Note that the results of its brainstorming resulted in subjects comfortable to the team members. In this case the subjects are typical of teenagers. The process is relatively simple and not beyond their competence even if some of the garbage measurements were yucky.

The use of NGT allowed the team to identify and agree on the problem, possible solutions, and recommendations. It is important that the people on the NGT team have the skills and knowledge to identify both problems and solutions. Team selection is vital to success.

MIDLAND CITY FULFILLMENT: WORK FLOW ANALYSIS/WORK SIMPLIFICATION

Carol Postman was grateful to Pete Ivers, president of Midland City Machine, for helping her start and nurture Midland City Fulfillment.

She had handled Midland City Machine's warranty and customer follow-up services for seven years. But when Carol's children were born, Pete Ivers allowed her to work from home. She eventually started her own office services business, which in nine years grew to 26 employees and some seasonal part-time help that handled a variety of paperwork and an entire warehouse of products.

Carol Postman had assumed her tightly knit crew comfortably shared ideas at employee meetings. But she found that teams on quality circles and statistical process control enhanced communication among her employees unlike any ordinary meeting. She was determined to find out why.

She held a special meeting to ask her employees for their opinions. She was surprised at what many of them had to say.

"When you spent time and money to train us, we believed that you really cared about our ideas," said Linda Fairlane, who worked in the warehouse.

"Before we had the training, we didn't know how to tell a good idea from a bad one. Now we're confident that we won't seem foolish or pushy when we offer our ideas," Carol's secretary said.

Training definitely would be an ongoing process at Midland City Fulfillment, Carol decided.

Carol Postman had become a true believer in suggestion systems too. While she had used the one at Midland City Machine, she really had no opinion about its real benefits at that time. But at Midland City Fulfillment, she actually could see the benefits of the citywide suggestion system, and her employees openly praised the system as a process that ensured that their ideas were carefully considered and responded to.

She wanted to continue her pursuit for quality and productivity by using another problem-solving process called *work flow analysis/work simplification,* but she was unsure whether her employees were up to another change. The process was particularly suited to analysis of paperwork flow and product flow—the primary functions of her business.

Carol first persuaded her key supervisors of the benefits of work flow analysis before she announced her plans to her surprisingly receptive employees.

"The process of change is logical and simple, but it requires dedication and an accepting mind," she told them, drawing on what she had learned from Deming's 14 management principles. "I'm pleased to have such dedicated employees!"

Clem Paxton, Carol's warehouse and merchandise manager, was eager to start the training with her. Through Midland City's adult education committee, they found a number of seminars suitable for their needs and ordered materials from Dr. Ben Graham, Jr. of Tipp City, Ohio. Ben was one of the primary providers of work simplification training and had developed a software product that simplified the charting.

Work flow analysis/work simplification calls for solving problems with a five-step approach: define the problem, break down the problem and visualize it in detail, question each detail objectively, develop an improvement proposal, and implement the proposal.

The process calls for the measuring of such factors as the distance walked, or the time that it takes to complete tasks. A systematic questioning of why, what, where, how, when, and who does the job helps to identify where improvements can be made.

After the two weeks of training, Carol Postman and Clem Paxton felt somewhat confident in using the process. Their instructor had used the layouts and data of their merchandise warehouse as examples to explain how the process works. That brought the process into perspective for them and gave them ideas for specific areas to work on.

Carol and Clem spent almost an entire day explaining what they had learned to Jenny Pilon and Helen Sikorski. Jenny, Carol's office and computer systems manager, would use the processes in her departments. Helen Sikorski felt the process could be applied quite successfully in the Midland City schools.

The process, Carol explained, uses a set of symbols that serve as visual aids in understanding work flow. Most problems are solved by a team of trained people that share common sense knowledge in an organized way. Work flow analysis requires learning a process during 40 hours of class time that helps understand problems and visualize solutions, Carol stated.

To start the process in the warehouse, Clem Paxton assigned his order fillers and packers to a team to analyze their jobs and determine areas where they could improve. To help determine whether the warehouse layout was efficient as possible, he provided them with pedometers, a device to measure the distances they walked to complete every task.

Jenny Pilon introduced the improvement process in her departments soon after Clem did in his. She took the advice of several of her teacher friends, who already were using statistics in their classrooms, and started the process by first determining what could be measured and what the measurements meant.

She had her employees list all resources they used to create specific products and services. She supervised keypunch operators, mail openers and verifiers, order reviewers, customer service people, and typists and stenographers. They compiled their lists at an early breakfast meeting.

"If we all expect to produce quality products, we need a way to define what that quality is," Jenny announced to her staff over coffee and sweet rolls at Tom's Cafe.

"Then our next step is to determine where our errors are occurring," she said to Gloria, her head keypunch operator. "The most critical keypunch output is making sure your people punch in the correct shipping set on orders. I want you to keep track of the percentage of errors you find on shipping sets each week and compare that number as a percent with the total number of orders that come to your department."

Jenny also asked the keypunch operators to measure the accuracy and legibility of orders they received from the order analysts. "Keep track of the ones you have to send back for clarification or rework," she said.

She asked the mail openers to verify that return addresses and coupons accompanied orders. She asked the order analysts to measure in percents the number of incomplete orders they received.

89

REVIEW OF WHO DOES WHAT

	Inputs	Outputs

Keypunch	Orders from analysts
	Inventory from warehouse
	Shipments from
	  warehouse
		Order/shipping label
		  sets to warehouse
		Reorders for merchandise
		  to Jenny

Openers	Mail	Verify return addresses,
		  presence of coupons,
		  etc., to analysts
		Inquiries to customer
		  handlers

Order Analysts	Verified mail from
	  openers
		Orders marked ready for
		  keypunch
		Orders with problems to
		  customer handlers

Customer Handlers	Problem orders from
	  analysts
	Customer inquiries on
	  problems
		Letters to customers via
		  word processing and
		  Dictaphone to typists

Typists	Dictaphone from
	  customer handlers
	Signed mail from
	  customer handlers
	  to mail
		Finished letters to
		  customer handlers
		  for signature

"Diane, I want your typists to keep track of the number of letters you have to redo each week because of mistakes by the customer service people. Keep track of who wrote them too," she said.

Jenny told them that everyone had to keep an account of the number of letters that had to be redone because of typing errors.

In less than a week Jenny began to see fewer errors because of her staff's effort to track them. She realized that some of the improvements were probably short term because they were immediate. She was well aware of the Hawthorne effect, where experiments in the 1920s showed that any change in operating practices will sharpen employee awareness and increase quality and productivity for a short time. It would be months before she knew whether the results were long lasting.

As more data were gathered, serious problem areas began to surface. Coupon redemption had the highest rate of errors. Jenny carefully read the redemption policies on the merchant coupons and found that they needed clarification. She established new rules for advising clients on how the redemption programs were to be handled.

The customer service department was another problem area. Some employees were having twice as many letters retyped as compared to the average. Jenny Pilon had just assumed all her customer service people were equally accurate. She decided to provide a training program to improve accuracy and to let the employees know what her expectations were. She also decided to post the data on errors so each employee had a daily feedback on quality.

All the employees found that the data pinpointed errors in their work methods or in their equipment. For most, the data helped to clarify their roles and responsibilities. The result was a 17 percent reduction in errors in order sets to shipping and improved work quality and productivity.

Meanwhile, Clem's order fillers and packers were progressing toward their own quality improvement goal. They had listed the steps to fill and ship orders and were ready to assemble and analyze their data.

Clem had taken on the role of work flow analysis task team leader and trainer. At the first meeting he explained how to use standard work flow process charting and, with his employees' help, he filled in the data on the time involved and distances walked to complete orders. He sketched the warehouse layout to help visualize what they were trying to determine.

Clem asked his employees to test each task listed on the charts with five questions.

- **What** are you trying to accomplish
- **Why** do you want to?
- **Where** could this be done better?
- **When** could this be done more effectively?
- **Who** is the best person to perform the task?

The work simplification team members found that many of their traditional roles and responsibilities fell by the wayside as they applied the questions to each task. They gained an insight into how they could use their resources more efficiently according to the warehouse floor plan.

The order fillers found they could eliminate wasted trips having the computer programmed to specify which merchandise to pick up in what order.

The packers found they could avoid unnecessary repacking by knowing beforehand what size box to use. They wasted at least 10 minutes every day repacking products they had tried to pack in undersized

WAREHOUSE AREA
EXISTING SYSTEM

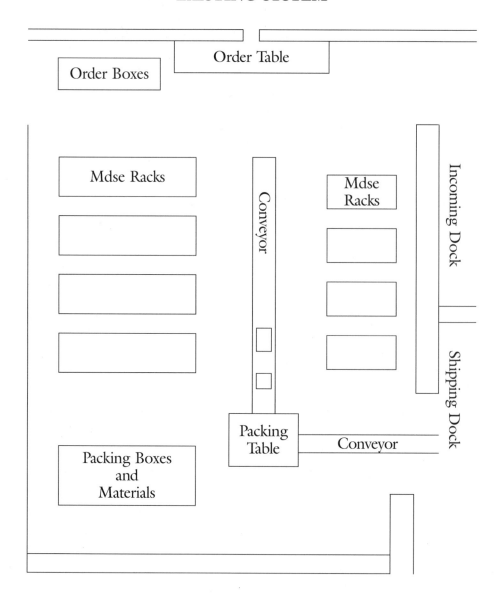

FLOW PROCESS CHART
EXISTING SYSTEM

Analysis
Why?

What?	Where?	When?	Who?	How?	Question each detail

Number		Page of

Job	Order Filler

Summary						■ Person	□ Material
	Present		Proposed		Difference		
	No.	Time	No.	Time	No.	Time	
○ Operations	5	0.7					Chart Begins
⇨ Transportations	5	1.9					
□ Inspections	3	0.9					Chart Ends
D Delays							
▽ Storages							Charted by — Date
Distance traveled	296 ft.		ft.		ft.		

Details of Method ■ Present □ Proposed	Operation	Transport	Inspection	Delay	Storage	Distance in effect	Quantity	Time	Eliminate	Combine	Sequence	Place	Person	Improve	Notes
1 Pick up order to be filled	●	⇨	□	D	▽			0.1							
2 Move to order boxes	○	◆	□	D	▽	20		0.1							
3 Pick up order box	●	⇨	□	D	▽			0.1							
4 Inspect order for sequence	○	⇨	■	D	▽			0.2							
5 Move to shelf for item 1	○	◆	□	D	▽	60		0.4							
6 Place item in order box	●	⇨	□	D	▽			0.1							
7 Repeat 4-5-6 2.6 times	●	◆	■	D	▽	156		1.8							
8 Verify order is complete	○	⇨	■	D	▽			0.2							
9 Move to conveyor	○	◆	□	D	▽	20		0.2							
10 Place box on conveyor	●	⇨	□	D	▽			0.1							
11 Return to order pickup	○	◆	□	D	▽	40		0.2							
12	○	⇨	□	D	▽										
13	○	⇨	□	D	▽										
14	○	⇨	□	D	▽										
15	○	⇨	□	D	▽										
16	○	⇨	□	D	▽										
17	○	⇨	□	D	▽										
18	○	⇨	□	D	▽										
19	○	⇨	□	D	▽										
20	○	⇨	□	D	▽										
21	○	⇨	□	D	▽										
22	○	⇨	□	D	▽										
23	○	⇨	□	D	▽										
24	○	⇨	□	D	▽										

Possibilities / Change (column headers above: Eliminate, Combine, Sequence, Place, Person, Improve)

FLOW PROCESS CHART
EXISTING SYSTEM

Analysis				
Why?				
What?	Where?	When?	Who?	How?

Question each detail

Number		Page	
			of
Job			
Packer			

Summary						
	Present		Proposed		Difference	
	No.	Time	No.	Time	No.	Time
○ Operations	13	2.7				
⇗ Transportations	7	1.1				
□ Inspections	3	0.6				
D Delays						
▽ Storages						
Distance traveled	113 ft.		ft.		ft.	

■ Person   □ Material

Chart Begins

Chart Ends

Charted by   Date

#	Details of Method ■ Present □ Proposed	Operation	Transport	Inspection	Delay	Storage	Distance in effect	Quantity	Time	Eliminate	Combine	Sequence	Place	Person	Improve	Notes
1	Remove tote box from conveyor	●	⇗	□	D	▽			0.1							
2	Move to packing table	○	◆	□	D	▽	20		0.2							
3	Determine packing box needed	○	⇗	■	D	▽			0.3							
4	Walk to box storage racks	○	◆	□	D	▽	20		0.2							
5	Select packing box	●	⇗	□	D	▽			0.1							
6	Return to packing table	○	◆	□	D	▽	20		0.2							
7	Assemble box	●	⇗	□	D	▽			0.5							
8	Insert merchandise	●	⇗	□	D	▽			0.5							
9	Add packing/padding	●	⇗	□	D	▽	10		0.5							
10	If box is too small	○	⇗	□	D	▽										
11	Repeat 3–9 5% of time	●	◆	■	D	▽	3		0.1							
12	If box is too large	○	⇗	□	D	▽										Est. cost 30¢ per oversize box
13	Excess padding and postage	○	⇗	□	D	▽										
14	Seal box	●	⇗	□	D	▽			0.2							
15	Affix shipping label	●	⇗	□	D	▽			0.1							
16	Move to scale	○	◆	□	D	▽	10		0.1							
17	Weigh—add postage	●	⇗	□	D	▽			0.2							
18	Place on conveyor to dock	●	⇗	□	D	▽			0.1							
19	Stamp shipping copy	●	⇗	□	D	▽			0.1							
20	Move to mail box	○	◆	□	D	▽	10		0.1							
21	Put copy in box	●	⇗	□	D	▽			0.1							
22	Place tote box on skid	●	⇗	□	D	▽			0.1							
23	Move to new tote box	○	◆	□	D	▽	20		0.2							
24		○	⇗	□	D	▽										

Possibilities / Change

boxes, and they had been wasting shipping and postage cost by packing goods in oversized boxes.

The packers found they could eliminate the reusable order boxes for collecting merchandise by programming their computer to specify the shipping box needed for each order and using shipping boxes to collect the order for placement on the conveyor.

The order fillers reorganized the warehouse merchandise into three groups: high, medium, and low usage. They stocked high demand inventory closest to the order pickup point, and they moved the conveyer belt from the middle to one side of the room to eliminate the need to run around it to fill orders.

The key was a new software program for keypunch operators to use for input in Jenny's area. Clem and Jenny found that by working more closely they could help reduce costs and increase the chances of adding new customers.

The new computer software system helped new order fillers work with accuracy.

After a few weeks Clem collected the calculations on time spent and distances walked. He plotted the results on new work flow process charts. He saw significant improvements in order filling and packing. Everyone in the warehouse had reduced the number of steps taken and were discovering ways to increase accuracy. With a more efficient warehouse, Midland City Fulfillment was able to operate with less overtime and to bid lower than competitors on new jobs.

Clem saw potential for significant growth. Once he had learned how to effectively plan and measure, working for quality seemed all so simple. He reassured his staff there would be no layoffs, even through he predicted that with increased efficiency he would have a 2.76 employee surplus. He reached that figure by multiplying the number of employees on a job by the level of improvement.

$$4 \text{ order fillers} \times 14\% \text{ improvement} = 0.56 \text{ person surplus}$$
$$4 \text{ packers} \times 55\% \text{ improvement} = 2.2 \text{ person surplus}$$
$$\text{Total} = 2.76 \text{ person surplus}$$

Clem assured his employees he would bring in more work to keep them all busy. After all, without their cooperation and work flow analysis/work simplification, he would have overtime costs and would have to bid much higher on new jobs.

Carol was ecstatic about the substantial savings available in what she had thought was already a modern, well-run, and highly competitive organization. She wasn't about to let anyone go.

WAREHOUSE AREA
PROPOSED LAYOUT

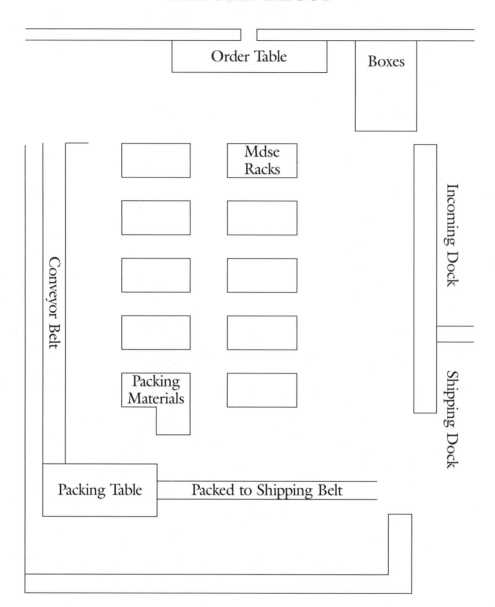

FLOW PROCESS CHART
PROPOSED SYSTEM

Analysis				
Why?				
What?	Where?	When?	Who?	How?

Question each detail

Number		Page of

Job
Order Filler

Summary						
	Present		Proposed		Difference	
	No.	Time	No.	Time	No.	Time
○ Operations	5	0.7	6	1.2	<1>	<5.>
⇨ Transportations	5	1.9	5	1.6	–	0.3
□ Inspections	3	0.9	1	0.2	2	0.7
Ɗ Delays						
▽ Storages						
Distance traveled	296 ft.		211 ft.		82 ft.	

■ Person   □ Material

Chart Begins

Chart Ends

Charted by   Date

Details of Method □ Present ■ Proposed	Operation	Transport	Inspection	Delay	Storage	Distance in effect	Quantity	Time	Eliminate	Combine	Sequence	Place	Person	Improve	Notes
1 Pick up order to be filled	●	⇨	□	Ɗ	▽			0.1							
2 Move to box storage	○	▶	□	Ɗ	▽	10		0.1							
3 Remove specified box	●	⇨	□	Ɗ	▽			0.1							
4 Assemble box	●	⇨	□	Ɗ	▽			0.5							
5 Move to specified shelf	○	▶	□	Ɗ	▽	40		0.3							
6 Place item in box	●	⇨	□	Ɗ	▽			0.1							
7 Repeat 5 and 6—2.6 times	●	▶	□	Ɗ	▽	104		0.1							○.25 ⇨.75
8 Verify order complete	○	⇨	■	Ɗ	▽			0.2							
9 Move to conveyor	○	▶	□	Ɗ	▽	20		0.2							
10 Place box on conveyor	●	⇨	□	Ɗ	▽			0.1							
11 Return to pickup	○	▶	□	Ɗ	▽	40		0.2							
12	○	⇨	□	Ɗ	▽										
13	○	⇨	□	Ɗ	▽										
14	○	⇨	□	Ɗ	▽										
15	○	⇨	□	Ɗ	▽										
16	○	⇨	□	Ɗ	▽										
17	○	⇨	□	Ɗ	▽										
18	○	⇨	□	Ɗ	▽										
19	○	⇨	□	Ɗ	▽										
20	○	⇨	□	Ɗ	▽										
21	○	⇨	□	Ɗ	▽										
22	○	⇨	□	Ɗ	▽										
23	○	⇨	□	Ɗ	▽										
24	○	⇨	□	Ɗ	▽										

Possibilities / Change

FLOW PROCESS CHART
PROPOSED SYSTEM

Analysis				
Why?				
What?	Where?	When?	Who?	How?

Question each detail

Number	Page of

Job
Packer

Summary						
	Present		Proposed		Difference	
	No.	Time	No.	Time	No.	Time
○ Operations	13	2.7	9	1.4	4	1.3
⇨ Transportations	7	1.1	4	0.4	3	0.7
☐ Inspections	3	0.6	1	0.2	2	0.4
D Delays						
▽ Storages						
Distance traveled	113 ft.		40 ft.		73 ft.	

■ Person ☐ Material

Chart Begins

Chart Ends

Charted by   Date

Details of Method

☐ Present   ■ Proposed

#	Detail	Operation	Transport	Inspection	Delay	Storage	Distance in effect	Quantity	Time	Eliminate	Combine	Sequence	Place	Person	Improve	Notes
1	Remove box from conveyor	●	⇨	☐	D	▽			0.1							
2	Move to packing table	○	◆	☐	D	▽	10		0.1							
3	Arrange merchandise	●	⇨	☐	D	▽			0.4							
4	Add padding as needed	●	⇨	☐	D	▽			0.1							
5	Seal box	●	⇨	☐	D	▽			0.2							
6	Affix label	●	⇨	☐	D	▽			0.1							
7	Move to scale	○	◆	☐	D	▽	10		0.1							
8	Weigh—add postage	●	⇨	☐	D	▽			0.2							
9	Place on conveyor to dock	●	⇨	☐	D	▽			0.1							
10	Stamp shipping copy	●	⇨	☐	D	▽			0.1							
11	Move to mail box	○	◆	☐	D	▽	10		0.1							
12	Put copy in mail box	●	⇨	☐	D	▽			0.1							
13	Return for new box	○	◆	☐	D	▽			0.1							
14		○	⇨	☐	D	▽										
15		○	⇨	☐	D	▽										
16		○	⇨	☐	D	▽										
17		○	⇨	☐	D	▽										
18		○	⇨	☐	D	▽										
19		○	⇨	☐	D	▽										
20		○	⇨	☐	D	▽										
21		○	⇨	☐	D	▽										
22		○	⇨	☐	D	▽										
23		○	⇨	☐	D	▽										
24		○	⇨	☐	D	▽										

Possibilities / Change

Helen watched carefully as the changes were made. Warehouse experience seemed to relate to custodial operations at the school. The office and computer activities related to the school administration operations. Helen could see real benefits in the process in a wide variety of organizations.

Leadership is evident in Carol Postman and her two supervisors Clem Paxton and Jenny Pilon. The process was selected at the top and led from the top. The use of work flow analysis (WFA) or work simplification lead to an orderly approach to problem definition and solution identification. The graphic presentation of data is a powerful part of WFA allowing the team, or the executives at a presentation, to readily identify the data, the relationships, and the validity of the solution.

Carol led her company to use an appropriate problem-solving tool, and she personally provided the leadership to ensure its success.

MIDLAND CITY
MACHINE:
VALUE ANALYSIS

Pete Ivers had been president of Midland City Machine for eight years, during which time his business nearly doubled. He was the largest employer in Midland City with 140 employees on the payroll.

Due to the size of his organization, Pete and his top executives routinely attended business leadership conferences and were well aware of the importance of effective management.

Midland City Machine produced a line of woodworking tools and machines for industrial cabinet shops and wealthier home workshop users. Ivers' products had become standard in schools and cabinet shops. But in recent months product costs were increasing, and Pete was losing ground to competitors who could offer their products at lower prices, particularly those who had plants in third-world countries where labor costs were a fraction of his.

Pete had to find a way to both increase sales and reduce costs, and he had to do so fairly soon.

Pete had his employees train for 56 hours in SPC and quality circles during a two-year period. The classes were held in the evening, and

Pete paid a standard hourly rate for the time spent in class to everyone who successfully completed the courses.

Overall, his employees welcomed the training, but some viewed the teams or circles as threatening. Pete's machine area supervisor felt teams would reduce Pete's authority and provide employees with a way to avoid directives; some of the engineers found using SPC troublesome. Having to set up charts for each machine, they thought, increased their work load unnecessarily, and they grew defensive as the resulting data began to uncover engineering and management as the source of 80 percent of the errors. They did not want to admit that they were among those contributing the most errors.

Pete spent a fair amount of time reassuring employees that the processes benefited everyone. Only seven employees were so negative that they were excused from the training.

Three months before they completed their training, Pete noticed that team participants had begun to take their roles more seriously than they had in the past. Early suggestions tended to focus on pet gripes, such as parking lot assignments, cafeteria food, and dirty rest rooms. But as the teams matured and learned to use SPC and NGT, the focus switched to product and process problems.

Pete was surprised that the teams' data paralleled Deming's predictions for all manufacturers. Nearly 80 percent of his company's errors were traceable to his professional staff, and only 20 percent were tied to machine operators and assembly workers.

The marketing and sales team used statistics to study costs and selling prices on all products. They uncovered several problem areas, most of which were traced to older product designs, especially the design of the wood lathe.

Pete suggested they use a method for design evaluation called *value analysis* to uncover ways to improve the design. Midland City Machine had been selling the same lathe for more than 30 years. Pete hired Roger Syverson, a value analysis consultant, to train him, the manufacturing supervisor, two engineers, and the sales, quality, and traffic managers. Once trained themselves, they would train the rest of the employees with the consultant's help.

Pete invited John Trock to train in value analysis because Trock Plastics supplied Midland City Machine's molded parts. Superintendent Sikorski asked to have one of her teacher/trainers participate too. The entire training team represented thinking on product design, customer needs, manufacturing, quality, shipping, subcontracting, and future training. A good combination, Pete reassured them.

The training took two weeks of half days. At the first session, Roger Syverson reviewed the history of value analysis. He said that value analysis, along with SPC and work simplification, was rarely used by Americans after World War II. American manufacturers had 20 years of market demand for everything they could produce so they generally ignored efficiency and quality measures. At the same time, however, Japanese study teams were eager disciples of the processes and had found effective ways to use them.

"In recent years," Syverson said, "the Society of Japanese Value Engineers has grown by leaps and bounds while American use of the processes has held steady—another indication of American complacency."

Syverson explained that value analysis has been used in medical offices and service organizations as well as in manufacturing plants. A brainchild of Lawrence Miles of General Electric Company, it was developed in 1947 to define the organized step-by-step process and techniques used to minimize costs in the design, development, production, and maintenance of systems or services.

"Thus, it purposefully forces a search for the best value in office procedures too," the consultant said. "It is not just a manufactured product design enhancement process, although it is particularly effective in that area."

Syverson used a number of case studies that he said would provide examples of the kinds of problems value analysis had solved effectively. One problem had to do with a purchasing department that had reduced paperwork and the time used to place orders. Another application involved encouraging vendors to generate cost-saving ideas. A third problem had to do with an insurance company wanting to increase the efficiency of its claims processing

After examining the studies, the team members were convinced they were learning a valuable and versatile tool.

Pete Ivers and John Trock noticed how value analysis, work simplification, and other problem-solving processes seemed to overlap. They were unsure of which one would best meet their needs. As usual, Arthur Black had an answer. They met with Black for lunch on a Friday.

As in almost any situation, Black explained, there are several steps in solving a problem. "You have to determine how big the problem is, where it is coming from, and any other details isolating the cause," he said. "Statistics, cause-and-effect diagrams, Pareto analysis, and process control charts are tools you can use to identify problems."

Correction involves an analysis using one of a variety of tools. Different problems can be better solved with the right tool. Black explained that there were applications of statistical process control, design of experiments, work flow analysis, and value analysis in different organizations in Midland City. He pointed out that there was another process, decision analysis, that was also known as the Kepner-Tregoe process.

Decision analysis is a method to help a group reach a suitable conclusion. In this process, all requirements or needs are identified as either *must* be done or *want* to be done. This effectively separates the group members' opinions and helps identify a solution meeting all of the musts and as many wants as possible. Decision analysis also includes other steps in reaching an optimum conclusion.

All of the processes help bring together all of the knowledge of the team in an understanding way, Black explained. Most of the problem-solving processes also create graphic representations of the data and the decisions.

"The processes must gain from the best ideas of all involved," Black continued. "Most stress team problem solving by employee teams or quality circles. A suggestion system provides a method for rewarding individuals or teams and provides a process for employees who tend to work alone to share their ideas.

Pete Ivers realized that he, indeed, was headed down the right path.

Syverson tailored his lectures on value analysis to focus on the redesign of Midland City Machine's lathe. Each part of the lathe, he said, had to be scrutinized by asking six questions.

1. What is the item?

2. What does it do?

3. What must it do?

4. What does it cost?

5. What else could do the job?

6. What does that cost?

Then he asked the team to review the lathe project against eight criteria to weed out steps that would not be effective use of its time.

1. Does the product need profit or cost improvement?

2. Will the product have a future of two or more years of active life?

3. Are sales forecasts and production schedules known?

4. Are documentation and cost data available?

5. Does annual sales volume warrant study expenditures?

6. Will technical expertise be available?

7. Will teams get management assistance?

8. Are hardware, prints, documentation, concepts, and work flow diagrams available?

The lathe had been designed in the late 1950s and was a slightly scaled down version of the heavy commercial machines used in industry. About 4000 of them were sold each year at a total of $1.2 million or 8 percent of the company's sales. The team determined that the current design of the lathe would be in demand for at least the next two years, but competitors were moving into the market. Midland City Machine seriously needed a new, more effective lathe design to compete.

The team members had gained the analytical tools in value analysis and had access to hardware samples and a wealth of consumer preference surveys as well as information about their competitors' products, including customer problem reports and several models of the competitors' lathes to dissect and compare. Their scope of analysis would have to be as broad as possible, Syverson said.

Using a chart, he reviewed the five steps of value analysis: the information phase, the speculative phase, the planning phase, the execution phase, and the reporting phase.

"The cardinal rules of information gathering are recording everything and challenging everything," Roger Syverson said.

The team diagnosed the lathe parts and scrutinized the competitors' models. The consultant then explained the functional analysis system technique (FAST), which calls for a detailed analysis of the costs and purposes of each part. They used a Pareto chart to analyze costs and usage of the parts, and statistics to help focus on areas where they could find the greatest value improvement.

The challenge of the speculative phase was to collect all their ideas for solutions and improvements. Syverson suggested that the team use the nominal group technique, a form of brainstorming that strongly encourages total participation.

He walked the group members through a creative thinking exercise to loosen their minds in much the same way athletes loosen their muscles before competing. The process was simple. The consultant held up a box of baking soda and asked the members to list all of its uses. Their answers included dozens of uses such as cooking, teeth cleaning, scouring, cleaning car batteries, and absorbing odors in refrigerators.

"How many of those uses do you think were part of the original baking soda marketing plan?" Syverson asked. "Would the product manufacturers have packaged and marketed the product differently if they had had those uses in mind?"

The team members, applying the exercise to the lathe, identified a variety of additions and changes, including varying the length of the lathe's bed to meet customers' needs, reducing the weight of the lathe to save costs in shipping and handling, and adding a work light.

JOB PLAN SCHEDULE
SET SPECIFIC PHASE DATE

MON.	TUE.	WED.	THUR.	FRI.	MON.	TUE.	WED.	THUR.	FRI.

Information Phase

Questions
1. What is it?
2. What functions must it perform?
3. What functions does it perform?
4. What does each function cost?

Techniques
- Define the functions
- Determine basic and secondary function
- Assign function worth
- Allocate cost to functions

Speculative Phase

Questions
5. What else will perform each function?

Techniques
- Blast—then refine
- Formal brainstorm
- Oversimplify
- Eliminate functions

- Sift results of brain-storm
- Put $ on every idea
- Establish alternate plans
- Assign work and set date for results

Planning Phase

Execution Phase

Questions
6. What else will perform each function?
7. What does each function now cost?

Techniques
- Refine results
- Evaluate by comparison
- Cost new ways to achieve functions
- Use standards

Reporting Phase

Techniques
- Show comparison cost (before and after)
- Be brief
- Be specific
- Specify action recommended
- Find and remove road blocks

In the evaluation phase, the team members determined the feasibility of each idea according to potential benefits and risks. They prioritized their ideas according to whether they would increase customer satisfaction, sales, and/or profits. They then determined if each idea was usable, unusable, or had possible future use.

During the development phase, the team reviewed the costs and savings that each of the selected plans would bring. Realizing that much of their reasoning was moving toward increasing customer satisfaction, they asked their marketing manager to join the team and arranged to have field representatives offer ideas and criticism.

After three months of applying value analysis the team members proposed a new lathe design. With the new design, they figured Midland City Machine could reduce the selling price of each lathe from

---

RECOMMENDED NEW LATHE

General Features

1. Maintains the same capabilities for doing quality work.

2. Reduces shipping weight by 40 percent.

3. Allows lathe ways to be sold in varying lengths to suit customer needs and work space.

4. Allows headstock to be configured for large bowl turning.

5. Allows easy belt replacement.

6. Promotes add-on sales.
   - Special stand
   - Variable-speed motor/drive
   - Duplicator attachment
   - Tool rests
   - Turning tools
   - Work light
   - Special tail stock for through boring

Design Details

Headstock
   Welded members with machining only on final bore for spindle bearings and mounting screw holes. Single end spindle. Ways mount into holes in headstock for rapid removal. Mounting point for work light included.

Ways
   Tubular steel ways supported by headstock and stamped saddle bracket at tail. Can be cut to any length. Easily removed from headstock.

$300 to $220, increase profit by $30 per unit, increase profit percentage of sales by 13 percent, and reduce the shipping cost per unit by $10.80.

At $220 per lathe, the team calculated, the company could sell 4000 more units a year for a total sales volume of $1.7 million and profit of $240,000. Sales for add-on parts, such as motors and stands, were total $820,000 for a profit of $82,000.

The company would gain a total of $2.5 million more in sales and $174,000 more in profits.

The team members became believers in value analysis. They had come up with major recommendations that would increase sales, profit, and customer satisfaction.

Pete Ivers was confident that the team had done its job carefully and anticipated few problems when he would turn the proposal over to the rest of the engineering and production teams for review and implementation. He celebrated by inviting everyone on the team to lunch to toast a job well done.

In this chapter, Arthur Black confirmed that Pete Ivers had chosen correctly by training in value analysis. Most management faces a major problem in deciding which skills to train. This is a major investment and must be done right the first time. Also, many executives have had exposure to many problem-solving and interpersonal skills processes that they found lacking.

Black convinced Pete that he was on the right track. Pete and the team then proceeded to apply value analysis with the result of a new lathe that will better meet customer needs and that will offer a major sales benefit to the company.

Here again, Pete was a leader in selecting the process and was a part of effective implementation. Management led both in the selection and implementation. This leadership is critical to both continued management support and employee involvement.

MIDLAND CITY
MOTORS

Bill Peterson considered himself a good businessman as well as a good mayor. Since he had taken over Midland City Motors from his father 16 years earlier, his work force had more than doubled to 30 employees.

He sold many cars to people in Meadan, the capital city 70 miles away. His overhead, taxes, and labor costs were low. His sales ranked fourth in the state for Oldsmobile dealerships and he could get the same volume rebates as the best dealers in Meadan.

But the local economic downturn began to take its toll on Midland City Motors too. New car sales hit an all-time low and repairs and used car sales went up. Fortunately, Bill had built a good repair and used car sales business based on fair prices, friendly service, and quality work.

He kept his repair shop open evenings and Saturdays and provided loaner cars to customers so they could go on with their business or pleasure while their cars were being fixed.

Bill wondered if his employees truly needed training in statistical process control and quality circles. He employed 12 mechanics, one supervisor, two people in the parts department, eight sales people, one sales manager, two clerical workers, one accountant, two janitors, and one driver to pick up parts. They had already developed a reputation for quality work and service.

How much could the processes help an already good operation? Bill wondered.

A lot, he found out.

Midland City's service industries started training 10 months after the strategic planning meeting. Bill's employees completed their training five months after that.

Bill assigned the sales, maintenance, and office employees to one team, which he called the office team, and the mechanics and parts people to another, which he named the shop team. The office team met every Tuesday morning for breakfast at Tom's Cafe. The shop team met at the same time and place on Thursday mornings.

Bill was surprised at what emerged after only a few meetings: His company's small town culture that seemed so open to communication was reluctant to point out the deficiencies of its neighbors. The employees definitely needed to learn how to talk about problems without being paranoid.

At Arthur Black's advice, Bill attended every other meeting of both groups, rather than all of the meetings. That way the employees could comfortably disagree with Bill's policies in his absence and gain his support on issues at the meetings he attended.

The office circle was charged with choosing the best merchandising methods for both new and used cars. Bill's sales representatives continually complained about insufficient showroom space and how cars were selected for the showroom.

"There's got to be a better way of selecting which cars go in the showroom than just allowing the sales manager to make that decision," said Julie Danielson, Midland City Motors accountant, at one of the office team's early meetings.

"Couldn't we use statistics to help influence sales and to help the sales reps close a sale on the first visit?" she asked.

The office employees skimmed through their data on how many of each car model and body type were sold each month nationwide, regionally, and at Midland City Motors. They tried to correlate the data with the cars that were displayed.

"One problem is that we do not change the showroom models on the first of the month," sales manager Lisa Raymond pointed out. "As a result, we cannot use the sales data to show how showroom display impacts monthly sales.

"I recommend that from now on we change showroom models to coincide with the sales data and study whatever impact that has on sales," she suggested.

Bill and the circle members agreed.

After six months, they compared sales of models that were not on the showroom floor to the sales of models that were. They calculated the sales impact by subtracting sales of models not on the showroom floor from those that were and plotted the results on a Pareto chart.

They were proud of the way they had used statistics. Some of the circle members thought they'd never understand how to use statistics or ever find a way to use them in car sales. Also, working as a team made them less at odds with each other. Working together on a problem gave them a new respect for each other.

Bill was amazed at the impact the showroom had on sales, even though he was well aware that impulse buying is a major force in car

	National Ranking Sales by	Average Sales						
SALES IMPACT								
Model	Model	Impact	Jan.	Feb.	Mar.	Apr.	May	Jun.
A (2D) Std	(1)	69.5 − 54 = 15.5	x68	51	52	56	x71	57
(4D) Std	(7)	20.6 − 12 = 8.6	10	x18	17	x21	9	x23
(2D) Del	(2)	22.0 − 17.6 = 4.4	25	x22	20	14	14	15
(4D) Del	(8)	19.0 − 12.75 = 6.25	7	12	x18	16	x20	16
			110	103	107	107	114	111
B (2D) Std	(3)	23.5 − 16 = 7.5	x21	16	15	17	16	x26
(4D) Std	(10)	21.0 − 13 = 8	16	x21	14	16	10	9
(2D) Del	(4)	22.5 − 18.5 = 4	19	12	x22	x23	21	22
(4D) Del	(14)	10.0 − 8.4 = 1.6	x10	9	8	7	10	8
(2D) Spt	(6)	27.0 − 17 = 10	14	x23	x28	20	x30	x27
			80	81	87	83	87	92
C (2D) Std	(9)	16.3 − 10.3 = 6	9	8	x16	x17	14	x16
(4D) Std	(13)	9.0 − 8.2 = 0.8	6	10	8	8	x9	9
(2D) Del	(11)	18.0 − 10 = 8	8	10	12	10	x18	10
(4D) Del	(5)	26.0 − 18.6 = 7.4	x26	21	16	x24	19	x28
(2D) Convt	(12)	1.4 − 1 = 0.4	x1	x2	x2	x2	1	0
			50	51	54	61	61	63

x = On floor that month

Calculation for average sales impact:
Average sales with display model − Average sales without display model =
Difference = Coverage unit sales improved average sales impact

UNIT SALES IMPACT FROM MODEL DISPLAY

0	5	10	15

Car Type

2 Door Std	A //////////////////////////
4 Door Std	A ///////////////
4 Door Std	B ///////
2 Door Std	C /////
4 Door Del	A ///
4 Door Std	B ///
2 Door Std	B //
4 Door Del	C //

/////////////////	2 Door Std C
/////////	2 Door Del B
/////////	2 Door Del A
//////	4 Door Del B
////	4 Door Std C
//	2 Door Convert C

sales. He knew his business was heavily impacted by showroom display because he had many out-of-town buyers who bought their cars during their first visit. From the office circle's findings he learned which models to show to maximize impulse buying.

The office circle members continued to explore ways to optimize showroom use. They wanted to present a plush image to their customers, but most of them came to Midland City for a bargain. If they found a bargain plus royal treatment, they'd surely come back to and tell their friends about Midland City Motors.

"We need to promote our services more," said sales representative Tom Newman during one meeting. "We could start by advertising our free loaner car service."

"And on rainy days, we could have valet parking for customers," said secretary Jill Jordan. "The customers could drive into the garage and the runners could park their cars so they wouldn't have to get out in the rain to shop for a new car."

Custodian Jerry Herman suggested they offer tours of the service area.

"Of course we would have to keep the area super clean, but the real benefits of the tours would be increased sales. Customers are influenced by a sparkling clean shop, you know," Herman said.

Tom Newman had one of the best ideas. He suggested that they use a new dealer emblem in chromed cast metal that would read "Quality Service by Midland City Motors." The emblem was right in line with Bill's beliefs in his company. He ended up ordering new emblems not just for new cars, but as replacements for the old emblems on used cars they resold.

Bill saw benefits in all the ideas. His repair shop was clean, but it was hardly a showplace. Besides, the insurance company discouraged allowing customers in work areas. But he agreed to suggest the tour idea to the shop team and arrange a joint circle meeting to address the idea.

The shop team's goal was to generate better quality and more efficient work in the shop while reducing costs. To review quality, four of the team members kept track of how fast and accurate shop work was done and the number of parts that failed before and after they had been installed. They documented each shop order that had to be reordered from the manufacturer and each part that had to be reinstalled.

They found that only 12 percent of all of the work done in the shop was rework, and 5 percent of the rework could be attributed to mechanic error. The rest of the rework was due to bad parts. The manufacturers of replacement parts that caused 46 percent of the problems only sold Midland City Motors 17 percent of its parts. Those suppliers had caused more than twice their share of errors and costly rework. Bill contacted the appropriate suppliers to resolve the quality problems. He brought his business to other suppliers when problems couldn't be resolved.

The shop team found that shop employees spent too many hours waiting in line for parts.

"Mechanics can't be waiting in line at the parts window, while the parts department hunts down parts and completes paperwork," said head mechanic Dan Riskon, at one of the meetings.

The team members discussed that problem at great length and toured several shops in Meadan for solutions. They had learned from their training that statistics had to be gathered with a vision of the probable result. With no data base to use in a statistical analysis of the problem, they had to find a way to envision the possible result and collect new data to be as efficient as possible.

First, they needed to know how each mechanic spent his or her day. They selected a process, offered by a consultant in Meadan, which involved taking a random time sampling. They gave a daily log form to each mechanic. At random intervals each day a Klaxon was sounded to signal that it was time for each mechanic to write an X and the time next to the description of the task on which he or she had been working. The consultant used a computer to analyze the data and reported the results to the mechanics weekly.

MIDLAND MOTORS MECHANICS
WORK BEING DONE IDENTIFICATION CARD

NAME _____ DATE _____

Working on repair							
Diagnosing problem							
Consulting on problem							
Assisting on repair							
Talking to supervisor							
Talking to parts department							
Making up parts list							
Waiting for parts							
Completing parts paperwork							
Completing work order							
Road testing							
Cleaning up bay							
On break							
Other							

After a month, it became clear that waiting at the parts department was taking up 11.6 percent of the mechanics' time.

At the recommendation of the shop team, Bill provided four mechanics and the parts department with two-way radios. The mechanics used the radios to order parts as they worked on or under cars. Thus, the parts department could have the parts ready when the mechanics came to the window.

The following month, the mechanics again logged their work as the Klaxon sounded. The results were significant. The four mechanics who used the radios spent only 2 percent of their time at the parts desk picking up parts. That was a savings of 9.6 percent per mechanic, or a 38.4 percent savings for all four.

Sometimes a mechanic wanted parts that hadn't arrived from the factory, hadn't been unpacked, or were at another dealership. The radios provided early notification to the people who worked the parts desk, allowing them to begin searching for parts before the last minute.

The outstanding results were enough to convince Bill to buy radios for all 12 mechanics. Some of the mechanics who originally had shunned the idea were quickly convinced otherwise. After all, they had an incentive program and were rewarded for jobs completed. They soon realized that the radios were just another tool for them to make money.

Bill had his office team members use the same random time sampling process in their departments. Their results were also significant.

Bill was eager to share his results with everyone in Midland City. He decided to share them with Bill Saxon of Saxon Motors—maybe not all the details on the showroom setup, but at least enough to tempt Saxon to design an emblem like "Saxon Motors, featuring Midland City Quality."

Midland City would not flourish with merchants battling over existing business, he rationalized. Midland City's future depended on its ability to bring in new business and to be recognized as having the best business climate in the state.

Bill had easily seen the use of statistics and problem solving for manufacturing. Now he had a chance to show others in Midland City that he was leading all of them on the right track.

Bill made logical moves in assigning teams with a specific area of focus. Note that with training in statistics the office group easily applied data gathering and analysis to a process they had observed for years. Their result was a better plan for showroom use.

The shop team quickly found bad parts as one of the major causes of errors and a Pareto approach led to changing suppliers to ensure better quality parts. Simple statistical technique led to effective changes.

The mechanics identified the problem of excessive waiting for parts. They invented a way of gathering data on what mechanics did during the day and could extend this into costs. Just like cost of quality data, these data gave Bill a reason to try a different approach that required some investment.

Through all of this there was Bill's support, as he attended every other meeting and implemented the good ideas of his teams.

LOCAL MERCHANTS

It was more than a year after the strategic planning meeting, and the citywide suggestion system was in full swing. Midland City residents were becoming increasingly aware of their right to quality. They disliked cold coffee, stale donuts, and shoddy clothing, and were no longer willing to pay for substandard products.

Many Midland City merchants originally felt they had no need for statistical process control and quality circles or teams. Most of them employed four to 15 people and believed that their employees already talked to each other on a regular basis.

After considering the numerous comments they had received, the merchants knew, whether they admitted it or not, that they had to improve their products and services. Bill Peterson stood behind the training 100 percent, and he had taken the time to convince the merchants that they and their employees would benefit from it.

The merchants' employees started their training a week after the factory workers completed theirs. Some of the younger employees had already been exposed to the processes at school and had a base of knowledge. Once they completed their training, their bosses assigned them to teams to look into complaints and suggestions.

Much of the criticism, both positive and negative, was directed to specific people and products. The teams used a combination of common sense and statistical data to identify the causes of problems and corrective actions.

Through the suggestion system, Tom's Cafe received numerous complaints about its milk shakes. For one month, owner Tom Rosterman checked almost every milk shake before it was brought out to the customer. The customers, however, continued to turn in suggestions for improvement. Tom asked his food quality team to look into the matter. The team members eventually uncovered and corrected the problem. They traced the complaints to Sundays and Mondays, the same days Tom was off. The assistant manager, who took over on those days, was a New York City native who preferred New York style milk shakes—thinner and sweeter—and made them the way he liked—not what local customers demanded.

Joe Carroll's problems at Clover Leaf Motel were much more serious. Carroll was lax in responding to numerous complaints about his dirty rooms and leaky plumbing. More than half of his rooms were usually filled because he had one of only two motels in town. But visitors to Midland City could hardly be impressed with the city's quality products or services if they slept in dirty rooms.

Bill, the five heads of Midland City's manufacturers, and two city council members met for breakfast one morning and decided to give Joe an ultimatum. Either he'd go along with the changes or they'd boycott his motel by recommending to their out-of-town customers and associates that they not stay at the Clover Leaf.

Joe grudgingly accepted the ultimatum. Bill and his team of manufacturers and council members randomly checked the motel for improvement. Joe at first was irritated by the spot checks, but it didn't take him long to learn that the costs of running a clean motel were outweighed by compliments rather than complaints from customers and the resulting increased occupancy. As he finally admitted, "You have to clean eventually so why not do it before someone gets mad."

Suzie's Dress Shop received several complaints through the suggestion system about shoddy merchandise. The complaints took Suzie Harold by surprise, even though she was aware that she was steadily losing customers to stores in Meadan. But she took pride in buying only what she considered quality brands and was surprised by the complaints on quality.

Most of the complaints were vague so she had the salespeople interview all the customers who had complained. They asked the customers what they specifically meant by "shoddy product" and why they failed to complain personally to Suzie.

Suzie and her staff finally traced 90 percent of the problems to one culprit—a brand of clothing with seams that more often than not split after only two or three washings. When the customers were asked why they failed to return the garments, they said that they didn't want to make a fuss and that Suzie was a friend.

Suzie realized that her friends had chosen to go elsewhere rather than confront her with a quality problem. For her, it had been an expensive lesson in human behavior.

Suzie approached the manufacturer with no success. "It's your problem to adjust the complaints. We have an image of quality," the manufacturing representative told her. Suzie immediately dropped that product line.

Better communication was the key to a quality image, Suzie decided. She sent a newsletter to her regular customers explaining what the problem had been. "Since our goal is to have only quality merchandise," she wrote, "I want you to *please* let me know whenever you have any problems!"

She decided to offer partial credit to customers who bought the bad products to compensate them for their loss. The customers were quite pleased with Suzie's honesty and generosity.

Good communication certainly paid off, Suzie concluded as sales began to increase.

All the merchants found using the processes to their benefit. Their employee circles uncovered needed changes in policy, buildings, and, in some cases, training.

Evan Lockwood learned that his dishwasher's backaches were caused by a sink installed four inches too low. Larry Anderson found that he was being taken by out-of-towners because his check-cashing rules were too confusing. Sally Severson learned that she could keep her employees happy by just supplying a paper cup dispenser so they could get a drink of water.

The merchants all benefited from the feeling of ownership their employees gained. Teams gave their employees a say in how they did their jobs.

Some of the merchants attended workshops on the other work improvement processes. Many of them felt that they would use work simplification to reduce their paperwork and to optimize their store layouts. They drew on the expertise gained by Midland City Fulfillment in work simplification. The process of change was not the chaos they originally had envisioned. Change was leading them to more customers, more profit, and happier employees.

The vision promoted in this chapter is that there are benefits for even the smallest businesses once they are aware of data gathering and analysis. Without data, we complain about results. With data, we learn to manage results. Suzie found out why sales were dropping. Bill put the pressure on the Clover Leaf Motel and increased visitor satisfaction. Data even pinpointed the cause of poor milk shakes.

In your organization, there will be departments that will insist that they are small and have great communications. Others will claim that learning statistical processes is not for them. We believe that learning to understand and use data is vital for all groups.

TROCK PLASTICS: DESIGN OF EXPERIMENTS

Trock Plastics produced a variety of injection molded and compression-molded plastic parts. John Trock's father, an expert mold maker, had started the business in the late 1940s and John took over when the elder retired. John, a natural entrepreneur, had tripled his business volume in only eight years.

But for the last two years, his business stabilized with no real growth. Competition was tough and costs were high.

Pete Ivers at Midland City Machine was one of John's best customers. Midland City Machine bought plastic parts for the woodworking tools it manufactured. The two men were close friends as well as dependable business associates.

John had eagerly joined Midland City Machine and the city's three other manufacturers to establish the quality image that Arthur Black and Bill Peterson had envisioned. John and his employees had established quality teams and were using statistical process control. They saw long-term benefits but also saw a lot of short-term confusion as they proceeded with the processes.

The suggestion system had been incorporated at Trock, and ideas were flowing into the city-managed system and immediately back to John's staff. He recognized the benefits of the system and set up his own system to handle the suggestions internally to reduce the response time to suggestions.

Three suggestions alone, he found, produced an increase of 2.6 percent in gross profit. The increase was well above what he had anticipated, so he was more than willing to pay the 10 percent of his savings to the city's quality program.

At the strategic planning meeting more than a year before, John had selected the concept of design of experiments as one that he would pioneer in Midland City. He and shop supervisor, Randy Clark, attended a three-day workshop on design of experiments in Meadan. It was an intensive course, and they devoted many evenings to studying the material after they got back to Midland City.

The instructor had pointed out the need to optimize a product design before it is released for manufacture. That means analyzing all the variables to optimize production and quality at the same time. Design of experiments does just that, the instructor explained. Once in production, statistical process control is the tool to measure and control variation of the product.

Design of experiments, which uses statistics to reduce the costs of experimentation, can be used to optimize interacting variables, the instructor said. She used an example for plastic molding to show the number of variables in a relatively small-scale production process.

INPUT VARIABLES— INJECTION MOLDING

1. Injection time
2. Primary pressure
3. Secondary pressure
4. Screw travel speed
5. Screw rotation speed
6. Mold temperature
7. Hot tip temperature
8. Bond heater temperature
9. Nozzle temperature
10. Cure time
11. Material moisture content
12. Material melt viscosity

Another example involved determining the best ratio of baking powder and baking soda in a cake. With two variables, the normal procedure would be to make four batches of cake with baking powder at the low or high end of the range and with baking soda at the low end of the range. Then two more batches would be run with baking powder at the high end of the range. These four experiments would be needed to gain data to select a best mixture.

Normally engineering schools teach the method of using tests of each combination of variations with one test at the top of the range and one on the bottom. With 12 variables and two tests for each possible combination, the number would be 2^{12} (or two to the 12th power) or 4096, the instructor explained. If all 4096 tests were run at a cost of $100 each, the total cost would be $409,600. As a result most indus tries use a high level of guesswork to determine the optimum combination of variables in a process. Using design of experiments to optimize variables would be much less expensive.

John listened intently as the instructor explained the history of design of experiments, which is sometimes called fractional factorial statistics. It was developed by agriculture scientists in England as a way to limit the number of planting years needed to produce hybrid seeds. Design of experiments allowed the researchers to limit the number of tests and thus reduce the number of experiments. The result was a reduction in costs and growing years to develop the plants.

John and Randy found the process straightforward but challenging. They knew they would be uncomfortable with the process until they had seen at least a few applications.

At the instructor's recommendation, they bought two texts and a video training package. The texts were chosen from offerings by ASQC Quality Press in Milwaukee, part of the American Society for Quality Control. The texts chosen were *Design and Analysis of Experiments* by Douglas C. Montgomery (Milwaukee: ASQC Quality Press, 1991) and *Quality by Experimental Design* by Thomas B. Barker (New York: Marcel Dekker and ASQC Quality Press, 1985). The video series was produced by Technicomp in Cleveland, Ohio. They felt that these books and the video would provide needed resources as they initiated use of this new process.

Trock Plastics needed to produce error-free plastic parts at the lowest cost possible. John and Randy decided to experiment first with the injection molding for tops of percolator coffee pots. The tops were produced in high volume and were frequently redesigned to change the appearance of the coffee pots.

Every new mold had a number of variables: the cavity shape, the gate size, the vent size, and so on. The consistency of the plastic, the temperature needed for molding, and the pressure and time needed in the mold were other variables. The company's long-time practice, based on judgment and experience, was to set up the molding press to an estimated best value for each variable. They adjusted variables until they ran parts to specification. Randy had a good feel for this and rarely had much scrap.

They decided to run their first experiment on the current percolator top model. The top ran two shifts five days a week with a 10-cavity mold. John Trock brought in an engineer from Meadan who was experienced in design of experiments. Both John and Randy were still unsure of themselves and happy to have help. The engineer worked for one of their customers who was eager to teach them what he knew.

The engineer said they first needed to gather basic data on how the part was running. He also suggested that they identify the cost savings and cost increases associated with each variable. They started by using data on quality measures from each cavity and on the history of the parts from a quality standpoint.

After they established a range of variance for each variable, they determined a fractional factorial design for the variables affecting their injection process. Those variables were gate size, injection barrel temperature, injection pressure, mold temperature, and cure time.

To find their optimal performance point, they normally would make three runs for each variable: high, medium, and low. With five variables, 243 runs would have been needed. At a cost of $150 per run, that process would have cost $36,450.

But by using design of experiments, they were able to approximate the optimal point in 16 runs at $150 each with a high level of accuracy. Using the process, they spent only $2400, a savings of $34,100.

John and Randy found they could reduce cure time 30 percent by decreasing the mold temperature 10 degrees, decreasing the injection barrel temperature by 15 degrees, increasing the gate size by 18 percent, and increasing pressure by 20 PSI. The total cycle for cure time was normally 40 seconds, so the 30 percent decrease reduced the cycle time by 8.4 seconds. The result was an increase in capacity of 21 percent. They produced more product per shift at a lower cost.

John and Randy were amazed at the increase in performance. The new molding parameters also offered more assurance of quality.

"Process optimization can give us a competitive edge both in quality and price," John said to Randy. "We can keep the company growing."

Another group of Trock's employees looked at ways to use statistical process control and quality teams. The office staff concentrated on improving order entry and order scheduling functions. One quality team carefully evaluated the causes of error with a cause-and-effect diagram and gathered data on each cause. After the employees finished collecting data, they constructed a Pareto diagram so they could visually identify the major causes of errors. They investigated the major causes to see how they happened and what could be done to prevent them from reoccurring.

The office staff recommended and made several changes.

- They asked for and were given new order forms that ensured completeness and accuracy.

- They requested that sales representatives be briefed on the proper procedures for filling out the forms and on what the costs were if the procedures were not followed.

- They reported all order errors in writing to John and the sales manager and kept cost-of-error data to track the total real cost of each order error. This data was shared weekly with all employees.

- They started a screening procedure using the computer to identify any changes in quantity, part number, or specifications from previous orders.

With the changes, the office staff found they had increased accuracy, reduced errors in the shop, and increased their efficiency in collecting outstanding accounts. Another outcome of the intensive data gathering was the pride generated as the employees' performance increased.

The several office teams in Midland City shared their experiment results. Bill Peterson was glad to hear the enthusiasm with which they reported on their projects and questioned each other for details. These monthly meetings of team leaders and members soon led to publicity in the *Press* with a result of other businesses getting ideas for improvement.

John reported his results with design of experiments at one of the manufacturers' Monday lunch meetings. The executives said they wanted to learn more about the process. Bill agreed to convince the adult education committee to sponsor a training seminar on the process.

Pete Ivers said he wanted to use the process. He was sure that it could help in his painting department where coverage problems and paint runs plagued the appearance of the machine tools shipped.

"I really feel that we've always been the best quality molders in the state," John told the group. "But now, we have a way to be the most competitive.

"We still have a lot of work ahead of us in training our employees in these new techniques," he continued. "Textbooks will become a part of everyone's evening and weekend reading, and I personally will lead discussion groups. Building more jobs and a new image isn't easy, but it can and will be done."

John's testimonial brought a round of applause.

Design of experiments gave a whole new vision to Trock Plastics. The process provided details on how to gain greater efficiency from expensive molding machines while increasing product quality. Trock was not unique in a lack of understanding or even awareness of this process. I have talked to many successful business owners with multiple variable processes who have never heard of design of experiments.

It is alarming that engineers and technicians still are graduated without awareness of this powerful tool. One does not need to be a competent practitioner to support occasional use. One must be aware of the benefits of design of experiments and have the courage to bring in a consultant to analyze a multivariable process.

THIRTY MONTHS

The day Arthur Black first spoke at the city council meeting seemed like a long time ago for most Midland City residents. They could barely remember what their city was like 30 months before. For most, it had been an active and exciting time of their lives. For some, however, it had been just plain exhausting.

Bill Peterson had been reelected as mayor, with the community threatening to make it a lifetime job. The majority of residents were 100 percent behind Bill and his vision. But Bill knew there were some, including his son, who believed he was leading them in the direction of a lot of work and expense with no assurance of success.

At the Peterson home, discussion during morning coffee and at the dinner table often accelerated to arguments over who in the family was doing more work. But each month saw stronger support for the goals of quality that Midland City and the Peterson family had adopted.

"How's your school work coming along, Scott?" Bill asked at the dinner table one evening.

"All right," answered Scott, who had just started his second semester of 11th grade.

"Just 'all right'?" Samantha asked.

"Well, you know we have to work awfully hard and we can't get by with just memorizing things. We really have to understand what we're taught. Our teachers have really gotten tough!"

"It's good for you," said Sarah arrogantly.

Bill frowned at his daughter as a motion to keep her sarcastic comments to herself.

"Doesn't it feel good to really be learning something and not have to fake it?" Bill asked.

"Yeah, but sometimes it hurts my brain to work so hard and sometimes I'm so drained that I can hardly play hockey."

"I doubt that. Nothing will ever stop you from playing hockey," Bill said half jokingly.

Meanwhile, Bill was pleased to find that Midland City's quality tax was a big success. Most businesses readily contributed 10 percent of their net savings that came about because they had successfully used statistical process control, quality circles, team problem solving, the suggestion system, and other quality control processes.

The tax generated more than $350,000 per year. *Midland City Press* reported the savings monthly and covered the deliberations and decisions of the board of advisors in charge of the money.

The advisory board funded several citizen programs to promote quality. An essay contest was held each spring for students in grades 6 through 12. The students submitted essays regarding the concept of quality improvement and how a community like Midland City could best plan and operate in the future using quality as a guide.

To gather background material for their essays, students visited local factories to observe the processes in action. Parents became involved in planning, proofreading, and sometimes typing the essays. The essays became a family project in many homes.

The essays were judged on how much research and thought they entailed, and if they offered clear, specific, practical, and affordable recommendations. Essays from students in grades six through nine were judged in one category; students in grades 10 through 12 were judged in another.

First-place winners in the younger category were awarded $200, and students who placed first in the older category were awarded $2000. All second-place winners were awarded $100 and all four third-prize winners were awarded $50. The winning essays were published in the *Midland City Press*.

In addition, if the essays were used and resulted in savings to a business, they would qualify for additional cash awards through the citywide suggestion system.

The first year—the year Sarah won first place for her essay—only a few students entered the competition. But the extensive publicity given to the winners prompted several more entries the following spring. At first editor Terry Brand worried that readers would be bored with the extensive coverage of the essays on the front page. But the publicity actually led to more subscriptions and street sales as relatives proudly bought extra copies that featured their sons, daughters, nieces, nephews, and grandchildren.

The citizen involvement programs emphasized upgrading the overall academic excellence and reputation of Midland City schools. Prior to Arthur Black's speech, National Honor Society meetings were rarely reported in the news, and few residents even remembered the names of past valedictorians. But for nearly two years, academic excellence was promoted much in the same way as athletics were in school and in the *Midland City Press*.

Students with a B average or better began wearing academic patches on their school jackets. Honor students held three meetings each school year featuring pizza, pop, and a special interest speaker. Students with C averages and who were showing significant improvement also were invited. The meetings proved to be an excellent way to involve marginal students in the quest for quality. Many average students found that being a part of the "brain trust" wasn't so bad after all and began to see the benefits of striving for National Honor Society standards.

The committee in charge of improving test grades provided transportation for honor students to the state university in Meadan and to plants in the city where they could explore career interests.

The names of honor students and students who were rapidly improving their grades were published after each school semester in the *Midland City Press*.

At the end of spring semester, photographs of all honor students of the year were a front-page feature in the newspaper.

Juniors and seniors were encouraged to work for at least a month in their career interest areas at local businesses. The committee subsidized the students' salaries to inspire the local businesses to hire the short-term student employees. The students had to write reports on their experience, and they rated the businesses according to how well it contributed to their career interest. The reports were graded and the students with the best reports presented them at all school assemblies.

Superintendent Helen Sikorski noticed that grades were rapidly improving and many of the discipline problems dissolved as more students took advantage of the programs. She anticipated a continuing rise in SAT scores as the younger students moved into high school.

The emphasis on helping Midland City grow was becoming an obsession with many.

With the money generated from the quality tax, Midland City had been able to send several travel teams to seminars and on tours of manufacturers and organizations that used quality improvement processes. The team members were selected carefully and the numbers were kept low. They shared what they had learned in presentations at businesses and the schools, and acted as consultants and advisers to the committee members.

Bill was pleased with how eager the manufacturers and organizations in other cities were to share information with Midland City. Most were impressed by how the entire community was moving toward a goal of a quality product for everyone.

After a few trips, Bill realized that the data gathering, particularly in Meadan, provided not only ideas for Midland City but also served as advertisement about what the community was doing. Two common questions from many outside Midland City were: "How is Midland City doing it? And how can you measure it?" Those people were especially impressed with how much money had been saved and the 10 percent quality tax that then yielded more than $350,000 annually.

Some large manufacturers in Meadan were using just-in-time (JIT) inventory management and total quality control (TQC). As Bill and the council members reviewed the processes, they felt they had identified the next phase for Midland City.

Bill was well aware that he and his people could learn about JIT and TQC by going to Japan, where the processes are used extensively. But he was convinced Midland City would benefit more by studying manufacturers in the United States and Canada, preferably present or potential customers, who used the processes.

Midland City established Commitment Day on the anniversary of Black's first speech in Midland City. The day was devoted to Midland City residents who had shown their commitment to quality. There was a city-wide barbecue in Bingle Park. In the afternoon, the committees presented reports on their accomplishments and their future plans. Terry Brand arranged for a special issue of the *Press* to commemorate the day with photographs of the committees and articles of their accomplishments.

Arthur Black, who was the honored guest, lavishly praised Midland City and said he was amazed at how rapidly it had improved product quality as well as its local economy. Bill and the city council members presented Black with a plaque with the inscription: "Key to quality— Midland City."

"You're absolutely right," Black responded with pleasure. "Quality is the key to every city."

He continued, "You have moved well down the road toward the goal of total quality management and toward your goal of recovering the prosperity you once knew. You have incorporated many of the basic statistical tools and problem-solving methods into your operations. However, there are new processes that need to be incorporated; like quality function deployment that will help focus on relationships of needs. You are at the start of a long journey of learning and applying new techniques that support your needs."

Black identified another goal for one or more local businesses: achieving a Malcolm Baldrige National Quality Award. He pointed out that winning would be fantastic but just the pursuit would be an education in effective management. Black suggested that one local business be selected to pursue the award with a team made up of other businesses helping. That way, the cost of pursuit could be shared and the learning spread.

Black predicted that a Baldrige award would be won in Midland City within two years. He offered his help to the team preparing the first Baldrige application.

That evening, two bands performed—a rock band for the young people and a country western band for the older residents. Fireworks topped off the celebration.

The next year, Midland City had a similar program with Black as guest speaker again. The winners of the essay contest read their papers during the afternoon ceremony, and a parade featured prizes for volunteer marchers who created a winning banner or costume bearing a quality slogan.

As they planned the third year's Commitment Day, Bill and his committee members decided to focus on drawing state and national attention to Midland City's accomplishments. By all measures, the local manufacturers were producing quality products. Both Trock Plastics and Star Electronics had achieved certified vendor status by their customers in Meadan, meaning their manufacturing processes were under statistical control to the level that their customers were guaranteed quality and could use the parts on their assembly lines without inspections.

Bill felt it was time to publicize what he liked to call "the miracle of Midland City." He knew publicity would focus many envious eyes on Midland City and fan the fires of competition. But keeping the accomplishments secret would not benefit Midland City.

The city council members established the Arthur Black Medal to present to the city's outstanding two quality teams. They had the medals mounted on plaques for the office or home and reproduced them in pin size for personal wearing. The two teams were rewarded also with all-expense-paid trips to a convention, of their choice, on team problem solving or statistical techniques.

To gain additional prestige, Midland City hosted a daylong conference on quality and productivity techniques, featuring Arthur Black and several nationally known speakers. Mailings on the conference were sent out nationwide through memberships of the American Society for Quality Control, the National Association of Manufacturers, the National Chamber of Commerce, and other professional organizations.

The conference was a big project for a relatively small community. But the committee members worked hard to attract the top names in productivity and quality processes.

Midland City residents were proud to host a national conference—the publicity was a big plus for the local merchants and manufacturers. The flyers printed for the conference cited examples of their accomplishments.

During the conference, a display area featured examples of the merchants' and manufacturers' parts and products impacted by statistics, circles, and the citywide suggestion system. The circle members were on hand to explain their successes. Midland City Machine's new lathe was a popular example.

A citywide cultural change had taken place in the brief 30 months, Bill explained to Rainville Mayor Ralph Huber during a round of golf in Rainville. Bill hadn't played golf for weeks because he had been so busy—he felt great to be back on the course. He was headed for a 40, he thought.

"The entire city has lined up behind the change process to make our community a growing one, not a dying one," Bill explained to Ralph as they walked to the second hole. "The process of understanding is part of the family, school, and business structure. It has become a fundamental part of life in Midland City. Even those who are not vocal supporters have contributed."

"But how do you know for sure?" Huber asked.

"We see it in class assignments and projects, in our suggestion system, in our circles and problem-solving teams, and at our annual picnics in the park," Bill answered.

Mayor Huber had difficulty understanding how Bill convinced his community to stand behind him.

"They all realized that what I was trying to do was for them, and now they are taking the initiative. The secret has been communication and recognition," Bill told Ralph. Bill explained how every successful organization needs to offer its employees a feeling of ownership and recognition and rewards for their work.

"Terry Brand has been a godsend for publishing our plans and achievements, and there have been several newsletters started in our companies and schools to recognize good employees. Our team meetings provide another method for sharing data. All this is supported by the local grapevine that carriers news at an unbelievable rate."

Bill explained how most businesses in Midland City offered cash rewards for usable ideas for improvement that came through the city-wide suggestion system. Other rewards for good ideas were emerging through a number of profit-sharing or gain-sharing programs. Some companies offered preferential parking spots to those employees who submitted good ideas. The cash rewards for essay contests and for outstanding teams also encouraged performance.

"We still have a long way to go, but we've come a long way," Bill said. He golfed his best game ever—a 35, one under par.

The vision is beginning to come together. It took a long time with the help of a lot of people. The schools are producing better graduates, and the quality tax is generating a significant amount of money. The vision of the community has created a process that raised money. The money is being used to further reinforce and expand the vision. Everyone is not ecstatic about the increasing amount of work involved. The work is justified, however, by the results.

Arthur Black is now expanding the vision to show Midland City that they are ready for new processes and pursuit of national recognition. At first the vision was kept at an acceptable level allowing people to reach a goal of competence. Now the vision is being expanded and Midland City is ready.

JAPAN: JUST-IN-TIME AND TOTAL QUALITY CONTROL

The three years since the strategic planning meeting had yielded results beyond Bill Peterson's wildest dreams. Every business that had used the quality control processes had profited, and the citywide suggestion system had induced millions of dollars in savings. Some defunct businesses were even reopening.

Still, Bill wasn't entirely convinced that sending a study team to Japan was in the best interest of Midland City. He knew the city could afford to send only a few people, and the average folks of Midland City wouldn't be chosen. He was afraid that a city-paid trip to Japan would be seen as a city-paid boondoggle for a selected few at the expense of an unselected many.

With the farm economy still on the decline, however, he knew Midland City had to find a way to create more jobs for farm families. He contacted various groups that worked with manufacturers seeking ideal rural locations. The organizations gave him the names of several manufacturers that had recently located in small communities across the country.

He conducted an informal survey of 25 manufacturers asking them what Midland City could do to better position itself for offers.

"We want our potential managers knowledgeable in just-in-time inventory management and total quality control," all of the manufacturers answered.

Fifteen of the manufacturers said they would seriously consider locating a plant in Midland City if its leaders were knowledgeable in and offered their workers training in the two processes. Several of the manufacturers strongly suggested that Bill take a study team to Japan to witness the processes in action.

With enough convincing from the manufacturers and city council members, Bill changed his mind. "The time is ripe for a Japan excursion. We have the need and good reason," he announced at a council meeting.

The week after Bill agreed to the trip, the *Midland City Press* featured an article, at Bill's suggestion, about the results of the surveys and comments from the manufacturers. The article addressed Midland City's need for more jobs for farm families, and quoted Bill's explanation of how the city could prosper by sending a study team to Japan. In the article, Bill asked for volunteers to help choose the study team members and to help plan the Japan itinerary.

Once again, Bill called Arthur Black for guidance. Black was able to offer invaluable advice because he had been to Japan several times.

In less than a week, 22 residents had volunteered to help plan the trip. Using advice from Black, they recommended that 10 people go to Japan. The selection was an even tougher problem. It was obvious that the business leaders were better educated and would probably gain the most from the visits. The team also knew that the quality process relied on involvement of all levels of employees. They decided to have the greater portion of the travel team be managers but still include some of the workers and technicians who supported the quality process.

The committee chose Bill; Helen Sikorski; Pete Ivers; John Trock; Randy Clark; Bill Willis, an engineer at Midland City Tool and Die; Betty Jacobs, a quality engineer at Midland City Manufacturing; John Hammer, a machinist at Midland City Machine; Norma Dahl, an office circle leader at Star Electronics; and Cheryl Jones, a quality circle facilitator at Midland City Fulfillment.

During their first meeting, a week after they were chosen, Black briefed the team on Japan's economic history.

"Much of Japan's modern posture began with the Emperor Meiji," Black began. "Meiji and other leaders, no more than 50 in all, began the original great cultural revolution in 1868. Before that, Japan had no modern business or industry."

Meiji led the first major change in 1868. General Douglas MacArthur started the second major change in 1945 when he introduced statistical process control, value analysis, work flow analysis, and other quality control processes developed in the United States.

World War II left Japan with a bombed-out industrial base and a nation with no real goals. The emperor-controlled government was gone and American forces had occupied its land. It was a nation unable to feed itself or keep warm on its own. The country desperately needed export income to buy food and fuel. Most of the world remembered a prewar Japan that exported cheap copies or inexpensive low-quality goods.

General MacArthur directed change in many aspects of Japanese life and businesses. He led the establishment of the kindergarten through grade 12 schooling equivalent we have in the United States with better control of courses and longer class times. He brought in Homer Sarasohn and Charles Protzman to lead the manufacturing of radios, telephones, and communications devices. Sarasohn and Protzman did better; they created a management and quality training system for Japanese executives that started the TQM process in 1946. Further consulting was provided by Deming and Juran starting in 1950. Japanese managers were taught to revere quality and respect competent workers during the same time that U.S. managers were ignoring both quality and workers in a quest for profit. In a sense, Black said, MacArthur and his people were humanizing Japan while U.S. managers were dehumanizing America.

"The U.S. corporations told the Japanese that they had too many financial people running their companies," Black explained. "They told them that they had too much bureaucracy, and they were paying too little attention to production workers on the factory floor and the quality of their products."

"Sound familiar?" he asked. "Well, the Japanese made use of that criticism and turned things around."

Black explained how Deming worked with the Union of Japanese Scientists and Engineers (JUSE) to establish the concept of statistical measurement.

Team problem solving was easy for the Japanese—their national tendency is to work in groups. Statistics, however, was new and posed quite a challenge. But the Japanese readily accepted the challenge. Japan's success didn't happen overnight, Black stressed. The Japanese worked vigorously from 1947 to 1977 before they perfected the processes that now dominate their production.

"But take note of Japan's lack of focus in such areas as merchandise distribution and agriculture," Black said. "In these areas, the country is far behind the United States. I want you to observe the good ideas without feeling that success is unique to Japan.

"Also, you must distinguish between mechanical and cultural differences in Japan. The United States can adapt most of Japan's mechanical processes, but many of the cultural persuasions are not suited for our use. Teamwork is one that we can learn to use. The lack of advancement of women and minorities in Japan are examples of where the Japanese culture is far behind ours. Also, Japanese employees are not free to move from company to company like we are here."

Black had several contacts in the Japan Management Association, a prestigious organization in Japan with a central staff of hundreds of people who analyze industry trends and provide training and guidance to Japanese businesses. He said the association would be willing to help plan and schedule the team's meetings and tours in Japan.

The study team members met with Black every other Tuesday evening for three months until they finished planning their itinerary.

Meanwhile, Midland City's citizens' reactions were mixed. Most people truly supported the trip, but a few scoffed at the idea and called it "the boondoggle of the year." To avoid further objection, the team members reluctantly decided against extending their stay in Japan for sightseeing. They also agreed not to bring their spouses, even on their own expense.

Black reassured the team members that going to Japan was the best way to further study the processes. They would return to Midland City more knowledgeable in the processes than most American business presidents, he said.

The team, Black stressed, had a good agenda. He warned, however, the Japanese companies rarely have women working in high-ranking positions, thus some of the companies could find it uncomfortable having to work with the female team members.

"I'm not suggesting that you change the makeup of the team," he clarified. "Just be aware that your hosts may be uncomfortable and act accordingly."

The day the team departed couldn't have been more perfect. The sun was shining and there was a fresh blanket of snow on the ground. The weather in Japan for the week, they were told, would be delightful but cold.

Few people other than families and close friends traveled to Meadan to see the team off at the airport. Samantha and several other spouses brought their cameras to record the departure. After all, it was the first trip to Japan for the team members.

Bill wished Arthur Black could come along, but he knew he was

fully capable of taking the lead.

The study team members hired an interpreter to serve as a guide, even though many of the larger Japanese companies had people competent in English. In keeping with Japanese tradition, they brought small gifts to present to their hosts at each company.

The 14-hour plane ride was exhausting The team members spent much of the time talking with the interpreter about what their week-long stay in Japan would be like.

They arrived at Narita Airport in Tokyo at 3:00 P.M. on Sunday. The taxi ride to the Capitol Toyku Hotel in the Akasaka district was interesting The taxi drivers drove faster than most New York cab drivers, and each cab was equipped with a door release lever that the cab driver controlled from the front seat. Bill, not understanding that he was to exit from the door that the cab driver had opened, exited the car on the opposite side—the traffic side—and received a citation. He learned the hard way that getting out of a car on the traffic side is illegal in Japan.

The team members were pleased to find the Capitol Toyku Hotel conveniently located near subway lines and with plenty of shopping and restaurants nearby. But they were disappointed in how expensive everything was. The food prices were frightening: $20 for a plain hamburger! But the restaurants, as were all Japanese public places, were impeccably clean.

They traveled to most of the plants by train and subway, the least expensive and fastest means of travel.

The five days of meetings and presentations passed quickly. Each evening the team members met after dinner to share what they had learned and to sharpen their lists of questions for the next day.

They attended a briefing on Japanese quality control. Bill previously had read much about the Japanese process in two books. One, *A Study of the Toyota Production System* by Shigeo Shingo, identifies the processes leading to just-in-time and the problems Japanese manufacturers faced in starting statistical process control. The other, *Guide to Quality Control* by Kaoru Ishikawa, details statistical process control methods and is considered a basic business textbook in Japan and America.

Japanese quality control calls for companywide quality control through education and training in quality control, quality circles, quality circle audits, statistical methods, and a nationwide promotion of quality control activities. The team members were already familiar with the six quality improvement steps, which were almost exactly what they had done at Arthur Black's direction.

"I've noticed a continuing indication of total quality control," Bill said after a visit to a plant that had done exceedingly well with Japanese quality control. "Each operator is responsible for the quality of his or her product, and each operator has the training, tools, and inspection equipment to do the job right the first time. I can see how, with the right quality checks, final inspection can be done essentially in an audit mode with a limited number of people."

The team members kept careful notes for Terry Brand who would prepare a "Japan Diary" for the paper after they returned to Midland City. They were disappointed that several of the plants would not allow cameras inside. In addition to the diary, they planned to produce a trip report and slide presentation. They took special note of the cleanliness and neatness in the factories, stores, restaurants, hotels, and trains. Japan is the size of Montana with a population that equals half of the U.S. population, the interpreter pointed out. Because it is so crowded, Japan has to keep things exceedingly neat.

Almost every factory they visited used just-in-time inventory or the *kanban* concept, which calls for producing parts only as fast as they are needed. Just-in-time eliminates the costs of inventory stockpiling and the risks of large rework or scrap costs due to error. A measure repeatedly used in Japan is the days of work in process (WIP).

Poka-yoke, the team members learned, is a concept of error proofing a machine, assembly, or office operation. Shigeo Shingo originated the process. Many Japanese manufacturers have used poka-yoke for years. It requires running a completed product through tests, measurements, or inspections that become an automatic measure to test and assure the product is correct.

Japanese companies used single minute exchange of dies (SMED) to allow rapid change of tooling in all types of machines. The rapid change cuts down on lost time during tool change, allowing a better control of quality with less inventory because runs are efficiently reduced. SMED is considered a fundamental process before starting just-in-time.

Helen Sikorski liked the way the Japanese quality circles operated. She felt her teachers would too, although they probably would not favor meeting 25 percent of the time on company time and 75 percent on their own time as most of the quality circles in Japan do. Maybe they would, she thought, if they were rewarded for their work as the Japanese quality circles are. Many Japanese circle members receive a cash stipend of $10 when they've completed a report or study. The report then enters a competition series. Winners are rewarded with a trip to an all-Japan conference and a JUSE-sponsored ocean cruise to Hong Kong or a trip to Hawaii.

The Japanese effectively staff and promote circle training, the team members learned. One company they visited had five promotion specialists and 10 trainers for 1300 hourly and 2200 salaried employees.

The team members were amazed at how effective the Japanese suggestion systems worked. They learned at a lecture that all companies had suggestion systems: some had systems to generate ideas only, some had value analysis systems, and others used suggestion systems to generate both ideas and solutions. With up to 100 suggestions per employee each year, the participation rate in Japan was 50 times higher than Midland City's.

Awards included value awards up to $1 for each idea submitted, but awards up to $5000 were possible for the best ideas. Tangible ideas were evaluated against a matrix of value of savings, creativity, and originality as measures.

Expectations for the suggestion system were discussed. The lecturer pointed out that even in Japan the change in behaviors to embrace the new concepts of quality and team operation was slow. "We were at this for 25 years before our market share really changed," he said. The next slide showed a 25-year history of the suggestion system at Toyota as an example of the reality of slow change. The lecturer also pointed out the continuous improvement in the suggestion process and stressed the need to plan for a long-term change. The chart on page 142 reproduces the Toyota data.

The team members were especially interested in how the Japanese companies used statistical process control. All Japanese employees are trained in the process, and it is used as part of their circle or suggestion system involvement.

During the factory tours, the team members were surprised to see few statistical sampling charts at assembly or machining stations. The teams learned that the preparation of typical $\bar{X}$ and R charts is costly, and usually these charts are reserved for a new product startup or particular problems. Some of the few charts they saw indicated quality acceptance at less than 0.002 percent error. The processes were definitely in control.

The concept of error proofing or poka-yoke is a process that provides 100-percent checks on piece parts. In one plant, the team saw a huge forming press making ½-inch diameter bolts for the automotive industry. The input to the huge press was 6-foot diameter coils of ¾-inch diameter stock. The forming press cut off a precise length from the coil and transformed it in four successive forming stations to a completed ½-inch bolt including hex head ready for thread rolling. The poka-yoke or error proofing was accomplished when every part slid down rails suspended from the head. There were measuring devices that verified the critical dimensions with automated sensors. If a part was out of tolerance, a gate dropped that trapped the errant part and the machine shut down. The gate prevented contamination of the other parts and the machine shutdown brought a team of operators on the run.

TOYOTA SUGGESTION SYSTEM 25-YEAR DATA

Year	Total of suggestions submitted	Suggestions per employee per year	% of employees participating	% of suggestions implemented
1951	789	0.1	8	23
1952	627	0.1	6	23
1953	639	0.1	5	31
1954	927	0.2	6	53
1955	1,087	0.2	10	43
1956	1,798	0.4	13	44
1957	1,356	0.2	12	35
1958	2,682	0.5	18	36
1959	2,727	0.4	19	33
1960	5,001	0.6	20	36
1961	6,660	0.6	26	31
1962	7,145	0.6	20	30
1963	6,815	0.5	21	34
1964	8,689	0.5	18	29
1965	15,968	0.7	30	39
1966	17,811	0.7	38	46
1967	20,006	0.7	46	50
1968	29,753	0.9	43	59
1969	40,313	1.1	49	68
1970	49,414	1.3	54	72
1971	88,607	2.2	67	74
1972	168,458	4.1	69	75
1973	284,717	6.8	75	77
1974	398,091	9.1	78	78
1975	381,438	8.7	81	83
1976	463,442	10.6	83	83
1977	454,552	10.6	86	86
1978	527,718	12.2	89	88
1979	575,861	13.3	91	92
1980	859,039	19.2	92	93
1981	1,412,565	31.2	93	93
1982	1,905,642	38.8	94	95
1983	1,655,868	31.5	94	95
1984	2,149,744	40.2	95	96
1985	2,453,105	45.6	95	96
1986	2,648,710	47.7	95	96

With poka-yoke the company could operate complex machines without operators in constant attendance. Bill and the team could see some real opportunities for this concept in Midland City businesses.

The use of poka-yoke required some advance planning for effective use of automated measuring. Pete Ivers pointed out that forms of poka-yoke had been in use in the United States for years. He was impressed that the Japanese were applying it much more widely than he imagined. Pete mused, "If all the parts I get at my plant were guaranteed by a 100-percent automated check, wow." Bill noted that the things they were seeing were what he had read about in Shingo's book.

The Japanese manufacturers had built quality into each part by providing designs that were not prone to failure. Further, there was a design for inspection and a design for producibility incorporated. Several of the team members were aware of training back home in these fields. It was obvious that this was another area of learning that they needed to consider.

John Trock was especially interested in how Japanese managers motivated their employees to take active roles in the processes. The managers provided much direction and required detailed reporting and measuring of the processes successes and failures. Several used company slogans to focus activity on specific goals for the month, quarter, or year.

Several Japanese managers commented on the impact of the United States' focus on high-asset returns. The United States seeks a 25-percent return on investments, while Japan seeks 5-percent return. The focus on high returns reduces investment, increases labor costs, and results in higher product costs, they said.

Bill noted that Japanese businesses, to their advantage, spend a higher percentage of assets than their U.S. counterparts do on robotics and automation. The auto company the team had visited was particularly impressive. But in some plants they saw machine lines that were obsolete or exceeded capacity needs by 10 to 1. Excess steel and shipbuilding in Japan are examples of planning problems, he said. Japan, they saw, was not perfect at everything.

The Japanese managers complained about the high costs of doing business in the United States. They blamed the costs on an increasing number of legal concerns with each business transaction, soaring costs of product liability, and employee lawsuits.

The team members pointed out the high cost of living in Japan. Japanese face high costs on everything they buy. Land costs are exorbitant and housing barely affordable. Few people have automobiles and fewer still would have a place to park one if they had it. Factory workers' salaries for major industries are similar to those in the United States and in some cases higher. There are, however, thousands of workers involved in small factories or cottage industries who live on low wages. The team also found out that Japanese executives and managers are paid far less than their American counterparts. This keeps the overhead on operations much lower and the businesses more competitive.

Another observation was that even made-in-Japan merchandise seemed more expensive in Tokyo than it would be if bought in the United States. Bill voiced his feelings that the Japanese may be beating us in the export game but he surely did not want to change places. Bill stated that what he really wanted was to live in a prosperous Midland City. Everyone agreed.

"We are lucky to be living in a country rich in natural resources and cropland, and capable of exporting most commodities," said Betty Jacobs. "Japan has to import almost 50 percent of its food, plus all energy and most raw materials."

"Americans must worker harder and produce better quality product for their salaries if they want to keep them," said Pete Ivers. He quoted Arthur Black: "American is changing—either we manage change or change manages us."

By Friday night, the team was exhausted. They had learned a great deal and had enjoyed their stay, but they were ready to go home to their families.

They spent much of Saturday taking in the Japanese culture. They rode the bullet train to Mount Fuji and had lunch there. The beautiful Shinto shrine next to their hotel was one of their favorite sights. That evening they went to the Ginza for shopping and dinner. They all bought gifts for their families. Some had grown so accustomed to the fresh kimonos provided in their rooms daily at the Capitol Toyku that they bought kimonos to bring home.

The flight on Sunday seemed to go much faster than it had a week before because most of the team members slept for nearly the entire 14 hours. Even Bill, who could barely wait to try out tempura cooking on his family, fell asleep an hour into the flight.

Benchmarking took on a new level with the trip to Japan. Bill was concerned that the money generated by the quality process should not be spent on a frivolous trip. Arthur Black was instrumental in persuading Bill that his team needed added vision to take Midland City to the next level. The Japan trip provided vital data and an enhanced perspective.

THE LEAD

The *Midland City Press* published the "Japan Diary" the Thursday after the study team returned home. The article was picked up by the Associated Press and it ran in the Meadan City *Tribune* that Sunday.

Bill Peterson couldn't have asked for more. The following week, the state coordinator for Apex Corporation called. She said she had read the article in the *Tribune* and wanted to know more about Midland City, including how many available workers it had. Bill decided to keep the inquiry quiet until it progressed to something more concrete. He didn't want to raise everyone's hopes, and he especially didn't want to stir up competition from other communities. Carter, only 60 miles away, had started to follow in Midland City's footsteps, and Bill didn't want Mayor Cohen to get wind of this too early.

Bill was confident that Midland City residents would welcome Apex and could supply the corporation with a host of exceptional employees. Most of the citizens were knowledgeable in quality control processes and had some experience in implementing many of them. Midland City would be a tough competitor in the contest for the Apex plant. Bill promptly provided the Apex representatives with the survey data that he had collected the year before on available workers. According to the survey, Midland City had more than 500 people looking for work, many of whom were only marginally employed on farms.

He and the city council members prepared a formal proposal on why Apex would benefit from locating a plant in Midland City. They sent the proposal along with the additional survey information to the Apex state coordinator.

Council member Dean Ostman continued to pursue other manufacturers, while Bill and the other city council members pooled their energies to win the Apex plant. Teamwork and dedication were really beginning to pay off.

Bill's efforts at publicity led Apex Corporation, a potential new business, to inquire about locating a facility in Midland City. Bill lead a team to provide Apex with the surveys and information needed to select Midland City. This is traditional marketing that most businesses do well. It is the steps leading to this point that American businesses are not doing. They are not identifying what it takes to satisfy the customer and they are not providing it. Too often we try to persuade the customer that what we've got is what they want. Midland City has done it right.

REACHING OUT

Bill was becoming a celebrity. The Apex plant moving to Midland City had attracted nationwide press, and the reasons for the Apex decision were well chronicled. Bill was being asked to speak across the state and even across the nation.

It was interesting to note that others were finding similar demands for their time. Helen Sikorski was a speaker at many educational meetings, and her model of using K–12 teachers and facilities as the focus of adult education gained a lot of recognition.

Pete Ivers and others in the manufacturing group were also finding demands for their telling of the Midland City story. Pete has also found that the notoriety of Midland City was a boost for his company's products.

Local merchants found that they were getting the majority of the shoppers who had the choice of coming to Midland City or going to nearby towns. The motels noted that there were a number of beds filled regularly with visitors who wanted to see how it all happened.

Bill found that the audiences he spoke to were much like what Arthur Black must have seen in his first visit to Midland City. Black had the benefit of consulting experience. Bill had the benefit of an example—of a community where it worked.

147

Bill noted that the audiences had a common bond. They recognized the threat to their community and the urgency of the need for a plan for both survival and recovery.

Bill found that he was most successful if he arranged his speeches around four points.

The Vision—This showed the audience what would be the path and the result of efforts to change. Midland City was the model.

The Imperative—This caused the audience to accept that change was fundamental to survival. Here the global challenge was discussed, and then Bill brought it down to terms for the community he was in. In showing the national deficit, Bill stressed, "Anyone is in trouble if they continually spend more than they take in." Bill asked the audience to state the increase in national debt and the balance of trade between the United States and Japan. A few members of the audience could and the numbers were written on a flip chart and discussed.

The Process—Bill used the chart Arthur Black had provided on how a factory works. Bill would point out that, whether it was a factory, a hospital, or his auto dealership, the relationships existed. Bill's use of examples from his auto dealership were well accepted by the listeners since they all owned cars and could relate to the ideas presented. Bill stressed management's roles of leadership as well as funding of the processes.

The Plan—Bill showed the audience the traditional PDCA (Plan-Do-Check-Act) cycle created by Walter Shewhart. The control circle showed the function of each component in the cycle.

- Plan—what you are going to do by determining your goals and the methods by which you plan to reach the goals.

- Do—what is needed to achieve the planned goals using the planned methods. This may require training or priorities to implement the work.

- Check—the results of your implementation of the plan and record all pertinent data. Evaluate data to determine if the goals have been met and which methods were used.

- Act—by identifying if objectives are met and if new objectives or goals are needed. Then start the entire cycle again.

Bill stressed the simplicity of this process and also the power of it. He urged his audience to carefully select simple processes to get them started and to have some measurable successes. Bill continually offered the option of a visit to Midland City to review what was done and what resulted.

The need for new skills was one of Bill's favorite topics. He could relate what he had learned and the benefits at length. His final visual "How to Succeed" was aimed at the community and business leaders.

CONTROL CYCLE

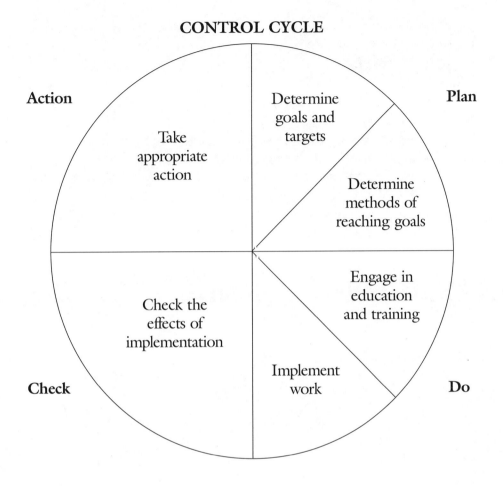

HOW TO SUCCEED

- Select the process best for your operation.
- Establish skills training relevant to each worker group.
- Insist that process be used and that ALL reports contain evidence of process use.
- Include in your directives evidence of your involvement in using the process.
- Have continuous training to expand knowledge of process techniques.

  Consultants • Speakers • Videotapes • Employee Success Stories Awards • Programs • Conference Participation

149

"Quality must become your way of life," he would say as he closed his presentations.

In four years, Bill had emerged as the Arthur Black to a whole new audience. The revival of Midland City coupled with his reputation as the mayor who instigated change spurred audiences everywhere to accept the points he made.

It wouldn't be too long before the leaders of other revived communities would be preaching change to others.

At home, life was never better. Sarah was in her second year of college on an academic scholarship, and Scott, a high school senior with a B average, had hockey scholarship offers from three universities.

"I'll never be a brain like you Dad, but it sure feels good to try," Scott confided in his father one morning.

"You never can tell," Bill reassured his son. "Look how far you've come in only four years."

The appendixes provide selected descriptions and reference materials to help you better understand how the processes used in *Recovering Prosperity Through Quality: The Midland City Story* work. The materials were also selected to provide a vision as to how you could use these processes and to help you select a starting point and a path to follow for your organization.

I chose to provide details on only Nominal Group Technique, Suggestion System, and Team Problem Solving since there is limited room in one book. I have provided references to authors who treat all of these processes.

There are seven appendixes.

- **Team Problem Solving/Quality Circles**—This is an expanded description of the process. It provides the needed team approach to problem solving.

- **Suggestion Systems**—This is also an expanded description. This process is easy to install and allows everyone to participate.

- **Nominal Group Technique**—This is another expanded description. It shows the step-by-step process of NGT.

- **Process Summary Charts**—These detail the operation of the following processes*:
  —Cause-and-Effect Diagrams with Cards (CEDAC)
  —Design of Experiments
  —Ergonomics (Human Factors Engineering)
  —Input/Output Analysis

---

*Reprinted or adapted from "A Performance Improvement Guide," Honeywell Inc. MRC 4-86-4.

—Just-in-Time (JIT)
—Nominal Group Technique (NGT)/Brainstorming
—Statistical Process Control (SPC)
—Team Building
—Value Engineering/Value Analysis (VE/VA)
—Visual Controls
—Work Flow Analysis (WFA)

- **Measuring Performance**—This appendix provides a description and examples of performance measurement in a variety of business situations.*

- **Performance Improvement Process**—The flowchart and accompanying description detail the seven actions needed for continuous process improvement.*

- **Definitions and Resources**—This is an expanded glossary providing definitions of terms and data on books and training available.

---

*Reprinted or adapted from "A Performance Improvement Guide," Honeywell Inc. MRC 4-86-4.

TEAM PROBLEM SOLVING/QUALITY CIRCLES

In *Recovering Prosperity Through Quality: The Midland City Story*, I have labeled the employee groups as teams or circles. To me, the terms are synonymous and this book could have been written either way.

Quality circles, as a title for team problem solving, has fallen into disfavor to the point that the International Association of Quality Circles has been renamed the Association for Quality and Participation. It is in recognition of this trend that this book uses team problem solving.

The term, *quality circles*, is alive and well in Japan. Its quality circles are the primary form of team problem solving. The term is still accepted and used in many businesses in the United States. The quality circle process, however, was so abused by management in many companies that it is not acceptable by either workers or management.

The following materials detail quality circles and how the process works. I did not modify this material since quality circles are team problem solving.

There are three general types of teams:

Title	Team source	Project source
Quality circles	Volunteer teams	Self-selected project
Quality improvement team	Mgt. selects team	Mgt. selects project
Suggestion team	Volunteer teams	Self-selected project

In addition to these basic characteristics, the three types of teams have some added features and benefits.

QUALITY CIRCLES

A quality circle is typically a group of seven to 12 workers who share a common process in their work. They meet for one hour once each week and identify problems and find solutions. They volunteer for the circle and pick their own problems. In many settings, the quality circle could last for several years. The circle is chaired by an elected leader and supported by a facilitator.

The benefits are in the sense of togetherness and continuity. The circles accomplish a lot with the traditional, basic statistical skills they use. Most organizations find that the circles saved more than they cost.

Problems arise from poor facilitating, poor management support, and the belief that the weekly meetings are a waste of time. The circles lose efficiency since all members do not have the knowledge, skills, or ability to create ideas to solve problems.

QUALITY IMPROVEMENT TEAMS (QIT)

Typically quality improvement teams are selected by management to solve a problem, which is chosen by management. The team may meet weekly or daily depending on the nature and urgency of the problem. The team usually disbands on completion of the assigned task.

The benefits are management support and usually the right people on the team to get the job done. The team also has clear focus on the issue and access to the problem-solving skills needed. The use of QITs is an excellent problem-solving process. The problem is that the team does not exist until management makes assignments. This assumes that management knows about all of the problems needing solutions.

SUGGESTION TEAMS

A suggestion team is usually brought together by an individual (peer) to solve an agreed-on problem. The team usually must meet on its own time and are eligible for awards under the suggestion system. Some suggestion teams may be allowed to meet on company time. Teams usually disband when the suggestion is completed.

The benefits are the ability of employees to determine problems they think need solving and to organize their own team.

Problems arise if the teams have no problem-solving skills and no member with leadership skills. Another problem is when data and interactions with resources must be done on company time; in this case, provisions must be made for a suggestion team to meet during work hours.

HYBRID TEAMS

There are many possible combinations and forms of teams. Some organizations use the output of visionary teams to identify problems in need of solutions. Teams form to solve a problem. Quality circles have identified issues beyond their scope and other teams form to pursue solutions. Suggestions may start as an individual initiative and grow into a team as complexity increases.

MANAGEMENT CONCERNS

A major management concern is the funding of a number of teams or circles all pursuing the same problem. Another fear is that the recommendations will come from a team without needed expertise or without logical problem-solving techniques. Both management and the teams want to approve the team recommendation the first time it is presented. This objectives requires that the team process be controlled as well as encouraged.

TEAMS NEED A PLAN

Almost all team meetings need a plan. This plan will perform several vital requirements. Approval of the plan will be required before problem-solving begins.

1. A clear statement of the problem is needed. Too often there is no common team understanding of the problem or issue. All problem-solving processes require that the team members first agree on the specifics of the problem.

2. What goals or strategies of the organization are supported? The team should be supporting the organization's goals. This may not be used if the organization does not have strategies or if they are not shared with rank-and-file employees.

3. What functions and skills are needed for the solution? Fixing a process or other error requires participation of people selected for their skills and knowledge. The team must include the needed expertise for a credible solution. The team does not need extras sitting in.

4. What steps and target dates are planned? Everyone needs goals and a team needs goals even worse than individuals. By publishing the goals and steps, communication between the team and management assures that priorities are matched.

5. What resources are needed and what are the anticipated costs? Definition of resources and a budget allow management to support or challenge the approach. Also, once management has approved, the team is assured of being able to complete the project.

6. Who will be on the team and what expertise do they provide? A list of the specific participants allows management the opportunity to assign added participants or otherwise adjust the team composition. Further, management may know of work priorities that could present selected team members from effective participation.

If all of your team meetings had a plan of this type filed, they would be a lot more productive. Also, you would probably eliminate over half of the meetings if the person calling for the meeting had to complete this plan first.

The team plan should be logged into a data base allowing all teams to be compared for conflict or duplication. The team schedule can be monitored and results summarized. Participation by individuals can be summed and reports allowing comparative participation provided.

The form on page 157 is useful to review a team's objective and plan for approval. This form should be used by quality circles, quality improvement teams, and suggestion teams. The data from teams can be combined with data from individual suggestions and summarized for employee involvement, support of strategies, process problems, and effective quality of work comparisons between departments.

Whatever their form, there is consensus that teams are needed to solve the broad process problems—those that cause 80 percent or more of the errors. Every organization must encourage teams. Every organization must also realize that everyone does not want to be on a team. There must also be a process for individuals.

THE QUALITY CIRCLE MOVEMENT

The first known circles in Japan were in 1962. By this time the imprint of Sarasohn, Deming, and Juran was made on Japanese organizations.

IMPROVEMENT PROJECT PLAN

What is the problem that you are planning to solve?

_____

_____

_____

_____

What strategy or goal does this support? _____

_____

What departments/divisions will benefit from a solution? _____

_____

What functions, skills, experience are needed for this problem?

_____

_____

What steps are planned in solving the problem?

Step 1. (Target Date _____) _____

_____

Step 2. (Target Date _____) _____

_____

Step 3. (Target Date _____) _____

_____

Attach detail if more than three steps are planned.

_____

What resources are required including costs?

_____ $ _____

_____ $ _____

Estimate completion date _____ Estimated savings _____

Estimated total cost _____

Team members

Name	SS Number	Skill they will provide

Submitted by _____ Phone _____

Control Office Check _____ Date _____

Team is approved for _____ meetings of _____ hours each and funding of
$ _____ . Team will provide progress reports at completion of each step. If team
anticipates increases in meeting time or funding, this must be required as early as
possible.

Approved by _____ Date _____   157

The circles provided an organized method for workers to combine their knowledge to improve quality and productivity on the job.

The work of Sarasohn started in 1946 with the establishment of manufacture for radio receivers. In 1948, it was clear that training in management and quality skills was needed. The creation of a focused MBA course for Japanese managers was the result. Two training classes involving 250 class hours followed. Added training in statistical methods was initiated when the Korean conflict erupted, and the focus was changed from Japanese recovery to war.

Dr. Deming in 1950 assured the Japanese that following statistical methods would result in their producing the finest quality of products in the world within five years. This happened, and the rest is history.

Dr. Juran joined the Japanese improvement process in 1952, and his concepts for management in the quality environment contributed added focus to the new industrial giant.

The growth of the Japanese quality circle (QC) movement was based on solid training in statistical methods and problem solving techniques. By 1960, there were over 100,000 circle members. Today, circle and team membership is in the tens of millions.

QUALITY CIRCLES OUTSIDE JAPAN

The success of the process began in the 1960s and rapidly covered the industrialized world. In the United States, the QC concept was first implemented by the Lockheed Company's Missile and Space Division. In 1972, Lockheed personnel visited Japan to study the QC process. The process was implemented at Lockheed in 1974 and within two years 30 QCs had been formed. An investment of $500,000 had yielded estimated savings of $3 million.

The process grew slowly for a few years and resulted in the first meeting of the International Association of Quality Circles that I attended in San Francisco in February, 1979. That first meeting of fewer than 200 people exploded into a huge organization within five years. Today, it is called the Association for Quality and Participation.

The process decayed, and my assessment is that the concept of measuring the savings generated against costs incurred was missing. Management will not long support any process that cannot prove a contribution to the bottom line. Our approach to teams and circles requires careful assembly of participants and an approved plan for operation.

Another weakness of the QC process is that a team that endures for years may lack the skills and knowledge to solve a wide variety of problems. Many circles I witnessed grew stale after many months. Some companies operated circles like teams with a "sundown clause." The circle was formed to solve a specified problem and then dissolved. My preference is for quality improvement teams to carry the majority of the problem-solving load.

The QC process had many attributes that are necessary to consider when setting up any teams. One technique I found most beneficial was the use of *action registers*. These listed all assigned actions that the circle determined, to whom, when to complete, and any other pertinent data. These registers allowed all levels in the organization to be aware of the process leading towards a solution. The register also provided a major incentive for circle members or outside resources to complete assignments. This is applicable to all teams.

QUALITY IMPROVEMENT TEAMS

The growth of QITs has been closely tied to the total quality management process. I can remember action teams formed to solve problems in the 1950s. These were essentially QITs but lacked the title. Many of these teams that I served on did not have the direction we prescribe in the included form. As a result, there was a lot of lost time, and most importantly, we could lack credibility when we presented our recommendations. I believe that all team processes must strive toward a "first pass acceptance" for the recommendations. Upon completion, the team is excited and proud. Deferring approval for another committee to review the findings deletes the joy and reduces enthusiasm for future team efforts.

My team approach takes this one step further in tracking the time of each meeting, the number of team members present, costs incurred in problem solving, and this total compared to savings. I believe that teams, circles, and suggestion systems need to be operated like a business, with costs and savings continuously compared.

GENERAL GUIDELINES FOR OPERATING QUALITY CIRCLES

These guidelines are typical of those proven for circle operation.

QCs consist of small groups of employees who voluntarily meet on a regular basis to identify, analyze, and develop solutions to problems, and to implement those solutions when feasible. This definition may be further clarified by a description of the common elements of quality circles—size, voluntarism, meetings, tool skills, and problem-solving methodology.

Size

QCs typically range in size between three and 15 employees, with the preferred size being at least five and no more than 10 members. If the group is too small, the interaction among group members tends to be limited, resulting in a scarcity of ideas. If the group exceeds 10 members, individuals are not usually afforded sufficient opportunities to participate, leading to apathy and disinterest.

Voluntarism

Workers typically are afforded freedom of choice in joining a QC. This freedom is an initial indication that management is committed to the concept. It is an indication both of how well management understands the QC philosophy and how deeply into the managerial structure the understanding has penetrated. When QCs are implemented on a voluntary basis, their achievements and benefits have a positive effect on the entire organization (given that the process has been properly implemented otherwise). The ultimate goal, of course, is that the QC process (Team Problem Solving) will become a way of life in the workplace.

Meetings

A weekly one-hour QC meeting is the rule, but there are exceptions, of course. Established QCs sometimes meet less often because subcircle meetings are held to discuss progress during information collection, solution development, or some other phase of the problem-solving process. Decisions about the meeting schedule and location provide management with an opportunity to demonstrate commitment. Meetings should always be held as scheduled. Frequent postponement of meetings communicates to workers that QCs are not important. This also applies to the meeting location. QCs must have a suitable place to meet and must be provided with the necessary supplies.

Tool Skills

During the problem-solving process, several tool skills are used by QC members. These are described as "simple statistical" tool skills. They can be subdivided into two categories: basic and advanced. Basic tool skills include brainstorming, cause-and-effect diagrams, check sheets, data collection, graphs, histograms, multi-vari charts, and Pareto analysis (see Team Problem-Solving Skills, page 162). Advanced tool skills used by QCs include control charts, sampling, and scattergrams.

The basic tool skills are taught to QC members during initial meetings. Six to 12 hours (meetings) are usually allowed for training in the basic tool skills and 12 to 24 hours for the advanced skills. The tool skills are at the very heart of the QC process, and it is important that QC members are well trained in their use.

Problem-Solving Methodology

The problem-solving process (identifying, analyzing, and developing solutions to problems and implementing those solutions when feasible) is basic to QC activities. After receiving training in the problem-solving process, QC members identify and develop a concise definition of a problem. The types of problems QC members attempt to solve range from simple housekeeping issues to complex changes in product or job designs.

The QC leader plays an important role in problem identification because if an intractable problem is selected, the group may experience frustration. Early success in solving problems helps to develop the confidence necessary for long-term QC effectiveness. Although the tools and techniques used are not complex, members unfamiliar with the structure and discipline of the QC process need time to adapt to them.

All members of the organization are invited to suggest problems for QCs to work on, but the choice of the problem must remain with the QC. This structure provides another opportunity for management to demonstrate support for the QC concept. If management selects the problems to be considered, the QC concept cannot survive.

The first step in problem solving is to identify, select, and define a problem. Then a method of measurement is selected. This enables a QC to know when the problem has been solved to the members' satisfaction. They then identify possible causes of the problem and collect data to identify the actual cause. Collecting the information required may be time consuming and difficult. The assistance of others in the organization may be needed to obtain the necessary information. In some instances, QC members use weekly meeting time to collect information rather than to meet in a group.

Once the cause of the problem is verified, a solution is developed. At this stage, the QC members have the opportunity to apply their knowledge and experience. (The QC concept assumes that the workers are experts at their jobs.) Controls are then established to prevent recurrence of the problem, and both the solution and controls are presented to management for approval. Upon securing approval, the QC members implement their solution. This is an important part of the process because it allows them to experience ownership in its fullest sense. Being deprived of this experience is detrimental to their participation in the QC process. Of course, there may be instances where it is physically or legally impossible for QC members to implement the solution. In such cases, members should be allowed to maintain as much contact with the implementation process as possible by assisting the implementors (as appropriate), and the group should be provided with feedback throughout implementation. Subsequent to implementation, the approved solution is evaluated to determine its effectiveness. If successful, the solution is standardized to the extent possible and shared throughout the organization.

A final step in the process has QC members make presentations to management about the effectiveness of solutions they have implemented. There are two purposes for these presentations: to provide the QC members with recognition for their contributions and (also important) to keep management informed of the progress being made by QCs. When a QC is newly formed and recognition is most important, presentations should be made routinely. As the number of QCs increases, it becomes impractical to formally present the details of every solution to management.

TEAM PROBLEM-SOLVING SKILLS

Brainstorming

Brainstorming is a method of creative thinking. The purpose of brainstorming is to facilitate unrestrained participation in the generation of ideas by all group members. Ground rules specify that any idea is acceptable. Group members share their ideas without evaluative comment from others. The rules that must be observed during the brainstorming session are as follows:

• Do not criticize anyone's ideas by word or gesture.

• Do not discuss any ideas during the brainstorming session, except for clarification purposes.

• Do not hesitate to suggest an idea, even if it sounds unrealistic. (Many times such ideas lead to a solution.)

• Take turns.

• Only one idea should be suggested at a time by each team member.

• Do not allow negativism.

• Do not allow the discussion to be dominated by one or two individuals. Everyone must get involved.

• Do not let the brainstorming session become a gripe session.

Brainstorming is useful during many phases of the problem-solving process, and is an invaluable tool in the QC process. In QCs, brainstorming is used for several purposes, depending on need. It is important that employees who are not QC members have an opportunity to contribute their ideas on the following:

- Problems to work on
- Possible causes of a problem
- Solutions to a problem
- Ways of implementing solutions

Cause-and-Effect Diagram

A cause-and-effect diagram is a means for collecting and organizing the possible causes of a problem. The diagram displays many causes but only one effect. The effect is the problem identified during a brainstorming session; it is what needs to be corrected or changed. The causes explain the effect; that is, they are the potential reasons why the problem exists. While there may be only one or two actual causes of the problem, there are many possible causes that could appear on the cause-and-effect diagram. The construction of a cause-and-effect diagram is completed as follows:

Step 1 Draw an arrow pointing to the right.

Step 2 Place a rectangle at the point of the arrow.

Step 3 Write the effect (problem) in the rectangle (for example, invoice errors).

Invoice errors

Step 4 Draw diagonal lines (branches) attached to the horizontal line and attach rectangles at the ends of the diagonals.

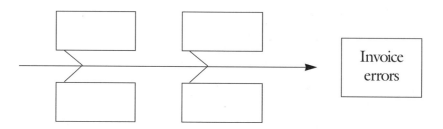

Step 5 Inside the rectangles, write the relevant categories.

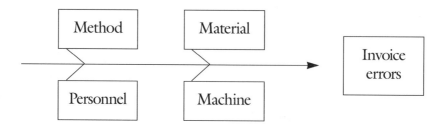

Step 6 Potential causes are identified by brainstorming. As they are identified they should be written on horizontal lines (twigs) attached to the branches. For example, when the causes of invoice errors are written on twigs, it might look like this.

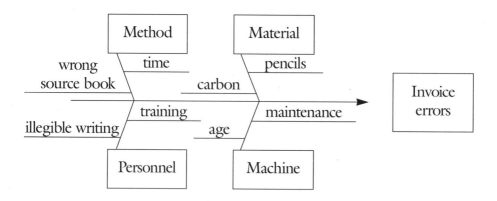

Check Sheet

A check sheet is a form for collecting information. For example, if additional information about a classroom is needed (see Pareto Analysis, page 167), the qualitative data collection check sheet might contain the following questions.

1. What activities take place in classroom E?
2. What type of supplies are required for those activities?
3. When, where, and how are the supplies needed in classroom E used?

Check sheets can take other forms, depending upon the information that is required. They can be used to keep track of job assignments, tasks completed, and scheduled activities in a QC, for example.

Data Collection

Data collection refers to the process of gathering information necessary to solve a problem. Check sheets may be used to record the information collected.

Data may be categorized as qualitative or quantitative. In problem solving, qualitative data collection is used to identify problems (that is, What's wrong?) and determine their extent (that is, When and where did it happen?). Quantitative data are usually collected to determine the exact cause of a problem. During data collection activities in a QC, the group is usually divided into subgroups to ensure full participation and maximum efficiency.

During the process of solving a problem, several methods of data collection will be used. The methods usually used are: questionnaires, personal interviews, observations, experiments, and record searching.

Graph

A graph is a diagram representing successive changes over time in the value of a factor. Graphs are constructed by plotting individual measures or averages at regular checkpoints. The following graph displays faculty absences for each month.

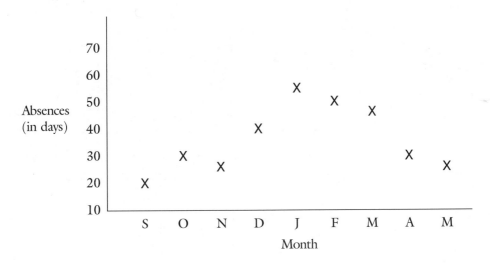

Histogram

A histogram is a graphic representation showing the pattern of data distribution. A histogram is constructed by first making a tally sheet and then replacing the tallies with rectangles proportional in height to the tallies. In the following example, the histogram illustrates the learning time in days of two classes, one using computer-aided instruction and the other using self-programmed texts.

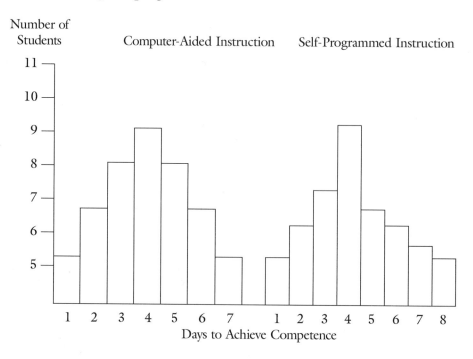

Multi-Vari Chart

A multi-vari chart is another type of graph used in data analysis. To illustrate, suppose injuries are reported at the end of each six-week period for students in automotive (A), building trades (B), and industrial (I) programs in four schools within a district. The data collected after 18 weeks are listed in the multi-vari chart shown.

Period	School											
	1			2			3			4		
	A	B	I	A	B	I	A	B	I	A	B	I
1	3	8	10	2	6	18	2	10	8	4	2	7
2	5	7	7	7	10	6	3	7	7	6	1	12
3	2	9	7	12	15	12	1	6	10	5	1	9

The multi-vari chart that results from the data is constructed by plotting a vertical line for each program (by school) that represents the range of injuries. The multi-vari chart enables one to observe (in this case) variation by school, by program, and within the same program across the four schools.

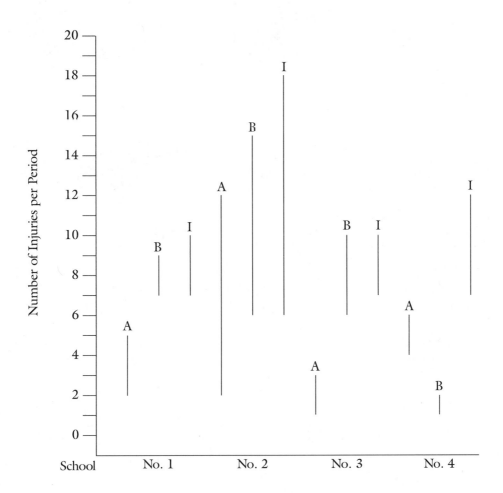

Pareto Analysis

Pareto analysis is a method of separating the most important characteristics from the least important characteristics of an event. It can be used to decide what problem to work on, to find the defect that has the highest cost, or in any other way that is useful.

Pareto analysis is a way of separating the vital factors from the trivial factors. The vital factors account for a large percentage of the effect. For example, suppose the weekly cost of supplies for eight classrooms is as follows:

Classroom	Expenditure		
E	$22.50	}	$32.69
B	10.19		(or 67% of the total)
C	8.16		
A	3.40		
F	1.50		
D	1.12		
H	.90		
G	.49		
Total	$48.26		

Classrooms E and B are responsible for 67 percent of the total expenditure. Classrooms E and B expenditures are the *vital* factors, and the other classroom expenditures are the *trivial* factors. Usually a few factors account for a large percentage of a problem and are therefore referred to as *the vital few*. The remaining factors are usually known as *the trivial many*.

Pareto analysis points to the direction for further investigation. In the example, classrooms E and B would be investigated to find out why their costs account for such a large percentage of the total cost of supplies. To make the vital factors readily apparent, the results might be displayed graphically.

The chart of this data would look like this:

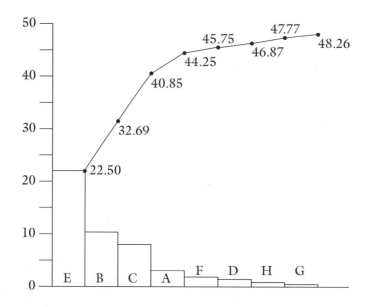

SAVINGS

Extensive documented savings are published from quality circles in the 1978 to 1988 time frame. The problem is that there is little real cost information to justify that the circles actually contributed to profits. My reviews show that circles did contribute to profit, but the data is not conclusive. Data on suggestion systems is better documented, and savings exceeding 10 times cost of operation are typical. We believe that the circle and team processes will be justified if proper planning is done and data accurately kept.

SUGGESTION SYSTEMS

Suggestion systems are controversial. The use of the process is again growing in the United States, but for every two new systems, there is one abandoned. The reasons are the same as for the other quality processes: lack of management support, poor process design, lack of ownership for the process, inadequate funding for administration and evaluation, and awards that are viewed as cheap or inadequate.

Included in this section are the following:

• A logical process for establishing a suggestion system

• A list of benefits from the process

• Some history and data

• Sample policies and procedures

A LOGICAL PROCESS

The objective of this process is to develop a suggestion system in which all participant groups have ownership. There are seven steps to the process.

1. **Set limits**—Top management must decide how much power and wealth it is willing to share. Sharing power comes from encouraging teams. And there is inherent power that results from team recommendations.

   Keep in mind that the suggestion process must eventually deal with awards that are consistent with the organization's compensation plan. Consequently, management must set limits first, so that a steering committee does not spend time developing a plan that is beyond acceptable limits.

2. **Select a steering committee**—The committee must represent management, evaluators, suggesters, operating supervisors, and the system's administrator or manager. The needs of these and other functions must be considered in the proposed suggestion system.

3. **Benchmark the process**—The steering committee must be educated and have all the information it needs to consider various options. Thus, visits to other organizations with good suggestion systems, training, conferences, and professional consultants are all resources that should be explored. A consultant allows all members of a committee to hear about the available options of a system. A combination of field trips and expert advice from a consultant are recommended.

4. **Analyze expectations**—This process identifies what each committee member expects from the optimum suggestion system. These expectations are enhanced by benchmarking which allows rational choices to be made.

5. **Define system details**—Through input/output analysis or similar methods, expectations can be organized. For instance, the type of reports issued, when they are issued, to whom they are issued, and similar decisions can be made. Since the reports determine what data is needed, the data defines what information must be collected on the suggestion form. Software becomes the tool for translating input data into output reports. (See sample input form on page 173.)

6. **Identify and present training**—The input/output process clearly defines the training needed for each participating function of the suggestion system. Thus, training must be defined and a training schedule presented in the kickoff plans.

7. **Continue support**—To ensure continued management support, the progress and details of the suggestion system must be regularly reported to management. Also, management must schedule time to present awards and recognize individuals and teams involved in the suggestion process. Standard software reports provide data proving the real contributions to profit of the suggestion system; this will also help ensure management's continued support.

Suggestion System

Supervisor Fill in
Last Digit of Year

Suggester Complete See Instructions & Eligibility Rules on Reverse Side of Suggester's Copy

☐ Individual　　☐ Joint/Team　　☐ Resubmit/Old Suggestion Number

Error, Problem, or Present Method:

	Sort Field #1　　Name
	Sort Field #2
	Sort Field #3

My Suggested Improvement (necessary to be eligible for cash awards):

Estimated Savings $

My suggestion is submitted for consideration under the Terms/Rules of the Company Suggestion System as set forth on the reverse side of this form. I understand such Terms/Rules and agree that the Company, subsidiaries, and its successors and/or assignees shall have the absolute and exclusive right to my suggestion including patents.

Suggester Eligible for Cash Award (Supervisor Complete)

1st Suggester's Name (Print)

Last Name	First	Mi	Employee Soc. Sec. No.	Dept. No.	Building	Mail Station	Division	Suggester's Signature	☐ Yes ☐ No

2nd Suggester's Name (Print)

Last Name	First	Mi	Employee Soc. Sec. No.	Dept. No.	Building	Mail Station	Division	Suggester's Signature	☐ Yes ☐ No

More than 2 on team – attach list.

ACTION SEQUENCE

**Supervisors MUST complete SUGGESTION Number and Date Received at the time of SUBMISSION, prior to separation of the copies. This is the LEGAL DATE of the Suggestion.

1. **Supervisor of suggester**—Determine investigator and fill in line (2) or complete disposition if within your scope. Separate copies and send to appropriate areas.	Supervisor of Suggester (Print)	Mail Station	Dept. No.	Date Rec'd	Date Sent	Time Spent	Initial
2. **Area team evaluators**—Clarify and evaluate the suggestion. Reach agreement on potential savings with suggester enter dates recd. and sent, time spent, and send to expert evaluator.	Investigator's Name (Print)	Mail Station	Dept. No.	Date Rec'd	Date Sent	Time Spent	Initial
3. **Expert evaluator**—Verify evaluation and savings. Request funding and implement suggestion. Measure savings, evaluate award and review with team. Complete sign-off line and send to suggestion office.	Second Investigator's Name (Print)	Mail Station	Dept. No.	Date Rec'd	Date Sent	Time Spent	Initial
4. **Controller/industrial engineer**—Support funding and installation of suggestion. Verify potential and actual savings for award. Date and initial.	Industrial Engineer (Print)	Mail Station	Dept. No.	Date Rec'd	Date Sent	Time Spent	Initial
5. **Supervisor of suggester**—Review disposition and if approved, date, initial, and proceed to line (6). If not in agreement, work with investigator until agreement is worked out.	Supervisor of Suggester (Print)	Approval of Evaluation ☐ YES ☐ NO		Date Rec'd	Date Sent	Time Spent	Initial
6. **Suggester notified**—Complete and send action (white) copy to suggestion coordinator.	Suggester Notified ☐ YES ☐ NO	Suggester Is: ☐ Terminated ☐ On Leave ☐ Transferred	Suggester's Signature _____				Date
7. **Policy committee**—Reviews major awards and returns to system manager to process check, plan recognition, coodinator schedules reviews, requests checks, and sends check and copy of action copy to supervisor.	Subcommittee/Policy Committee				Date Rec'd	Date Sent	Date Complete

Investigator/Industrial Engineer Complete & Return to Suggester's Supervisor

Disposition (be specific):

FOR ADDITIONAL SPACE AND SAVINGS CALCULATIONS USE REVERSE SIDE OF THIS COPY

☐ Adopt	Date Installed	☐ Not Adopt	Date Not Adopted	NOTE:	Supervisors/Investigators: Keep the system updated on suggestion status. Submit update form when suggestion moves or investigator changes.

Suggestion Office Complete

Gross $ Saved	Cost to Implement	Net $ Saved	$ Awarded	Add on $	Date Completed	Award Type ☐1 ☐2 ☐3 ☐4

BENEFITS FROM THE PROCESS

Measure the Benefits of New Skills

Problem-solving skills are vital to correcting complex problems and processes. Encouraging employees to find solutions eventually leads to recognizing the need for more skills. Training employees in problem-solving skills is costly. This is where the suggestion system can help. It there is a question of which of several skills would be best, it is possible to train each skill in a different area and measure the relative value in savings.

Encourage Use of Problem-Solving Skills

Frequently problem-solving skills are taught and little is done to ensure their use. As a result the training goes stale, the investment is wasted, and the employees see another management foible. The suggestion process can be established so the use of the new skills creates a bonus. For example, if work flow analysis is trained to all employees, then any suggestion with an accompanying WFA chart will gain a cash bonus if the idea is used.

Management Support

The suggestion process must provide management timely data on all aspects of the system. Management needs to know if the process creates a profit or if it operates at a loss. They want to know who did what so that should recognition is appropriate. They want to know which departments and individuals support the suggestion process and which of the organization's strategies or goals are tracked through the suggestions. The suggestion data offer many options for enhanced reports to management.

Profit Center

A suggestion system should operate as a profit center. It generates validated savings and compares savings with costs involved in evaluation, administration, implementation, and awards. Data show that suggestion systems in the United States generate significant savings. These are often equal to four times what is costs to run the suggestion system. Some systems save even more money.

Without operating data, complaints about the work involved can obscure the real savings. Yes, suggestion systems cost money to operate. But they also create more profit for less money than other possibilities.

Create a Team Atmosphere
Teams can be used to create, evaluate, and implement suggestions. Further, teams can identify needed training and, in some cases, present it. If suggestions are reviewed by peer evaluation teams, this simultaneously generates ownership of the process and builds skills. Implementation teams can be used whether ideas come from individuals or teams.

Show Variance in Quality of Work
The data can be organized to show where errors come from and the total number of errors created by each department or division. Thus variation can be identified and corrective actions can be taken. Data can also be organized to show which processes or products caused the errors. Here again, the variance can lead to corrective action.

Keep in mind that the data based on errors found and corrected is, statistically, not a proper sample. With reasonable amounts of data, however, the appropriate conclusions can lead to suitable corrective actions.

Empowerment
In order for employees to be empowered by the suggestion system, they must believe the following:
- The organization wants the employees' ideas.
- The organization will treat the employees' ideas with dignity.
- Employees will not be threatened because of their ideas.
- The organization will provide timely answers to employees' suggestions.
- Management will fairly share the wealth and power with employees.

The modern approach to a suggestion system (see page 176) will ensure empowerment through carefully designed rules of operation and through management's involvement to ensure integrity.

Promoting the Individual
Creative, motivated, hard-working people are sought for promotion. In many organizations, the active suggestion system participants are frequently promoted to lead or supervisory assignments. The data in the system supports promotion. The publicity these employees receive validates their promotion to their peers.

SUGGESTION SYSTEM BENEFITS

Rewards

Team problem
solving

Individual
problem solving

Recognition

Promotability of
the individual

A modern
suggestion
system

On the job
training

Measure benefits
of new skills

Empowerment

Show variance in
quality of work

Encourage use
of problem-solving
skills

Create a team
atmosphere

Profit center

Management support

Recognition

The book *The One-Minute Manager* by Kenneth Blanchard, Ph.D. and Spencer Johnson, M.D. (New York: Morrow, 1981) stresses praising as a part of employee communication. Most managers are concerned that when they praise an individual, others in the department might feel alienated. The modern suggestion system removes this worry. The awards *earned* are validated by the supervisor, the suggester's peers, and the appropriate technical review. The financial savings to the organization are well documented. Since the savings are real, management can pour on the recognition without worry.

Rewards

How much reward? The answer is simple. How much will it take to cause people to change behaviors and submit their ideas? The answer is also complicated in that a lot of great ideas are generated for a short time without monetary awards. The Hawthorne effect will guarantee short-term results. Cash or merchandise? Both kinds of awards have benefits. Experience shows that over a period of a few years, a mixture of cash and merchandise will probably have the greatest results.

HISTORY/DATA

The suggestion process started in Germany in the 1800s and spread to the United States just at the end of that century. It fell out of favor after World War II when there was little focus on employee involvement. Slow response to evaluation, management reluctance to spend money for awards, and administrative costs were key factors.

In recent years the advent of low-cost personal computers has created new options. Data can be manipulated and sorted in exciting ways, thus making the process easier to use. Also, the data combined with that from quality improvement teams allow focus on support of strategies and identification of errant processes.

The Malcolm Baldrige National Quality Award has provided a stimulus to suggestion systems. Suggestion data support proof of employee involvement in change and can show specific support for published strategies.

There is a lot of available data. Data all support the fact that suggestion systems will make money and improve employee involvement if they are properly established and supported.

The following data show the United States far behind Japan. The award-winning suggestion system at Honeywell generated more than three suggestions per eligible employee, five times the National Association of Suggestion Systems average. In Japan, there are businesses where over 100 suggestions per employee per year are received.

Organization	Suggestions/Employee/Year
Average of EIA-member organizations	0.6
Best year, Honeywell Defense Systems	3.2
Japanese-owned U.S. factories	Up to 12
Japanese companies (1991 data)	
Best	426
Approximate average	40

SAMPLE POLICIES AND PROCEDURES

The following is a sample policy. It contains more rules than you may wish. It is intended as a shopping list that you can edit. It will serve as a reminder of details you need to consider when you develop your organization's policies and procedures.

SUGGESTION SYSTEM POLICIES AND PROCEDURES FOR CASH AWARDS

Foreword

This procedure outlines the current policy and procedure of the Suggestion System. It has been developed and approved by members of the Board of Judges to maintain consistent application of the Suggestion System. The information is considered Company Property, and you are asked to return your copy to the Administrator of the Suggestion System when you are not directly involved in the operation of the Suggestion System.

1.0 Scope

This procedure covers the objectives of the Suggestion System, the duties and responsibilities of personnel in administering the system, and the rules and procedures for implementing the system.

2.0 Objectives

Objectives of the Suggestion System are to provide:

- An organized method for all eligible employees to submit constructive ideas on matters that are beyond the normal expectancy of their duties or responsibilities.

- An investigation that is unbiased, consistent, prompt, and efficient.

- Benefits for employees whose Suggestions are adopted and constructive, tactful rejection of unacceptable ideas accompanied by the reason for rejection.

- A follow-up that ensures all personnel involved directly or indirectly with the Suggestion System are performing their functions properly and that all benefits from this system are being realized.

- A Suggestion System that assists in improving the economic status of the Company.

3.0 Organization

3.1 Board of Judges

A Board of Judges governs the Suggestion System.

3.1.1 Membership. The Board of Judges consists of five to seven members. These members are representatives obtained on a rotating basis from all departments.

3.1.2 Responsibilities. Responsibilities of the Board of Judges are to:

- Provide an organized method by which employees can submit constructive ideas for managerial analysis and, if the ideas are accepted, receive monetary awards.

- Provide a method of evaluating employee Suggestions that is unbiased, consistent, prompt, and efficient.

- Interpret and clarify Suggestion rules and eligibility requirements.

- Propose changes and amend rules, with appropriate Management approval, to increase the effectiveness of the employee Suggestion System.

- Review Subcommittee recommendations for all awards over $300 and take final action.

- Assume final authority on its decisions relative to the awards to be paid by the Suggestion System, including the denial of any award or eligibility for an award.

- Establish Subcommittees as required and appoint Subcommittee members.

- Delegate duties and responsibilities to the Subcommittees in such a way as to establish and maintain a fully effective Suggestion System.

3.2 Subcommittees

3.2.1 Membership. Subcommittees are all made up of qualified people obtained on a rotating basis from departments, and they are appointed and maintained by the Board of Judges. No more than one new member is to be appointed to a Subcommittee in any three-month period. Subcommittee Chairpersons are appointed by the Board of Judges.

3.2.2 Types of Subcommittees. Subcommittees could be:

- The Office Subcommittee, which deals with Suggestions from nonexempt Office and Technical employees.

- The Factory Subcommittee, which deals with Suggestions from hourly paid Factory personnel.

- The Toolroom/Maintenance Subcommittee, which deals with Suggestions from those areas.

3.2.3 Responsibilities. The responsibilities of Subcommittee members are to:

- Maintain a consistent policy in applying the Suggestion System rules in the Factory, Office, and other areas as assigned by the Board of Judges.

- Review all approved ideas.

- Determine final disposition of any idea entailing an award of $300 or less.

- Act as arbitrator in any dispute between personnel as to the validity or feasibility of a Suggestion.

- Request, if required, the actual personnel involved in a dispute to appear before the Subcommittee until a decision is reached.

- Aid in establishing rules of operation.
- Act, at the request of the Subcommittee Chairperson, as special investigators or in assisting concerned supervisors to evaluate ideas.

3.3 Administrator

The responsibilities of the Administrator of the Suggestion System are to:

- Maintain a Suggestion System Procedure Manual, which contains guidelines for consistent interpretation of policy and rules in the Factory and Office areas. Any changes to this manual must be approved by the Board of Judges.
- Coordinate the administration of the system with the Investigators, the Subcommittee, and the Board of Judges.
- Maintain the records necessary for efficient functioning of the system.
- Coordinate the investigation of Suggestions in such a way that a fair and logical conclusion can be reached on each idea.
- Analyze the backlog of Suggestions.
- Prepare reports of the effectiveness of the Suggestion System to management.
- Act as employee representative at the meeting held by the Board of Judges.
- Aid in review of all appealed Suggestions.
- Prepare data for Board/Subcommittee review.

4.0 Rules of Eligibility

4.1 General

To be eligible for cash award, a Suggestion must be submitted by an eligible employee or eligible employee group on an eligible subject beyond the normal expectancy of the suggester's duties or responsibilities; and it must recommend an action which, when adopted, will result in a saving or improvement to the Company. Employees will not receive awards for carrying out their work assignments.

Employees in the trades (electricians, machinists, plumbers, carpenters, general maintenance, tool makers, tool designers, technicians, and so on) are employed specifically to utilize the arts and skills of their craft and to apply them to maintenance and repairs of buildings, machinery, and equipment. They are expected to use their knowledge and experience to avoid recurrence of a breakdown or a condition calling for their assignment to this specific job or area.

If the Suggestion is outside the job scope or the work assignment, the Suggestion is eligible for award.

4.2 Eligible Employees

All factory nonexempt employees, including part-time employees, and nonexempt administrative personnel are eligible, with the exception of the Suggestion System Administrator. The company controls the right to determine the classification of the exempt/nonexempt employees.

4.3 Eligible Subjects

4.3.1 Types of Subjects. Subjects that are eligible for Suggestions include those that would result in:

• Savings in time, material, scrap, rework, or tooling

• Improvements in products, safety, or working conditions.

• Elimination or reduction of layout or paperwork errors where cost savings are involved.

• Improvements in systems or in procedures that are performed in regular established systems for record or cost purposes.

4.3.2 Limitations on Eligible Subjects. Some limitations, primarily of time, are involved in submission of Suggestions on eligible subjects. These include the following:

• Subjects must pertain to equipment or methods formalized by layouts or written operating procedures. Informal methods or oral instructions are not valid subjects for Suggestions.

• All products manufactured or methods used by the factory will be eligible for Suggestion 90 days after layouts, inspection procedures, prints, and/or designs are originally issued. New tooling, equipment, and machines installed on the production floor and ready to run production parts will be eligible for a cash award 90 days after qualification and/or production acceptance. There are no time limitations on safety ideas. Eligibility prior to this date would be at the discretion of the Manager. This would be formalized by a memo from the Manager to the Board of Judges.

• Ideas for salvaging parts are not eligible for a period of two weeks from the date the parts are rejected.

• The Suggestion must be submitted within 15 days of the time it was mentioned or first used in the department.

4.4 Ineligible Subjects and/or Proposals

Subjects that are ineligible for cash awards include those that:

- Pertain to routine maintenance such as repairing worn tools or equipment, installing, moving, or cleaning lights, plumbing, paint work, and the like.

- Deal with Company policy or managerial decisions such as negotiated labor contracts, employee benefits, public relations, recreation, parking program, and the like. It is a matter of Company policy or managerial decision to decide if and when jobs are to be run in the plant or subcontracted; therefore, sourcing ideas are ineligible and not open to Suggestions.

- Concern motivational programs, publicity, or slogans.

- Pertain to proposals already under active consideration by the Company.

- Apply to inspection procedure revisions dealing with sampling plans.

- Concern feeds and speeds.

4.5 Time Suggestion Is Valid

A suggester's idea is protected, if properly submitted, until such time as an award is made or the suggester is notified that the idea is not acceptable. If a Suggestion is not approved when submitted but is put into effect within two years from the date of rejection, the employee has the right to bring his or her original Suggestion up for award. All Suggestions shall remain active for two years from date of decision. Such suggestions may be resubmitted before expiration of the two year period if the idea still seems to be of value or if it has been implemented.

5.0 Investigation of Ideas

The Investigator and Implementing Supervisor must carefully and impartially evaluate each idea, taking into account all savings factors.

5.1 Types of Ideas

In general, Suggestion ideas fall into the following categories:

Cost reductions—for example, savings in labor, materials, machine hours, downtime. Some questions to ask here are, does it:

- Substitute machine operation for hand operation?

- Reduce personnel hours for operation?

- Reduce or eliminate materials use?

- Save energy?

- Reduce work load for rental machines?

- Substitute less costly materials?

- Reduce waste?
- Increase output per machine?
- Prevent breakage or prolong life of tools, equipment, or machinery?
- Improve design or function of equipment?
- Change tools or equipment to reduce manufacturing time?
- Change flow of materials to eliminate unneeded operations?
- Combine forms?
- Combine operations to reduce costs?
- Improve handling and storage?
- Save paper or other supplies?

Product improvement—that is, any idea that betters the quality, performance, appearance, construction, or utility of our product. Questions include:

- Are defects reduced or eliminated?
- Is eye appeal improved?
- Is product more dependable?
- Will performance of device be improved?

Safety—that is, ways to reduce accidents or fire hazards. These ideas may involve:

- Calling attention to unsafe practices.
- Recommending installation of guards.
- Use of protective clothing or equipment not normally available.
- Fire prevention measures.

Convenience—that is, changes that make a job easier or more pleasant, although there are generally no tangible savings involved, and which would have a direct effect on improving employee morale.

5.2 Recording Information
Investigation information is recorded on the ACTION COPY in "Disposition" block on the front of form, on the reverse side of the ACTION COPY, or on a suitable attachment to the ACTION COPY. The report is completed by the Investigator with sign-off by both the Implementing Supervisor and the originator's Supervisor. In those cases where there may be some doubt as to whether or not the submitter's suggestion is within or outside of his or her job scope or responsibility, the immediate Supervisor must make a preliminary decision and obtain concurrence and sign-off by the next level of supervision.

5.3 Investigators

An employee's immediate Supervisor is responsible for investigation of the Suggestions. Responsibilities include:

- Investigation of Suggestions and/or coordinating the investigation with other personnel who can best evaluate the specific idea.

- Assurance that investigations are fair and impartial.

5.4 Sequence of Investigation

The following sequence should be followed in investigating an idea submitted as a Suggestion:

- Read and analyze idea.

- Recommend disposition (accepted or unapproved).

- Approve or obtain approval of Implementing Supervisor.

- Evaluate savings factors of accepted ideas and submit to Industrial Engineering for verification.

- Submit to Suggestion Office.

5.5 Investigation Procedures

The following are the major procedures that should be observed in investigating and evaluating Suggestions.

In reading and analyzing an idea:

- Check the basic schedule and estimate the value of the idea to determine how much time should be spent on the investigation.

- Estimate dollar expenditures required to put idea into effect.

- Approve idea or contact Implementing Supervisor to discuss its merits—that is, the economics of installation and the savings possibilities.

Practical ideas should be put into effect as soon as possible:

- Contact the necessary people for action.

- Explore related applications.

- Notify suggester if use of the idea is to be delayed 30 days or more.

- Establish a tickler file to remind investigators to follow up action.

Evaluate cost savings—An acceptable Suggestion must result in a cost savings or be of positive value to the Company. Implementation cost is not deducted in arriving at the annual savings for award calculations. All implementation costs should be recovered within one year (capital equipment is an exception to this rule), or the idea is not economically justified. Calculate the hours saved by comparing the new method to the old using approved rates. Estimates will be required when approved rates are not available.

Determine the gross savings for one year—Evaluate all savings factors. Find hours saved by comparing new method to old using time for a normal operator at 100 percent performance in both instances. The labor rates (do not include burden) to be used for savings calculations are obtained from the Suggestion Administrator.

Evaluate material saved—for example, quantity reduction in paper usage or cost reduction by use of cheaper form or brand of merchandise.

Evaluate reduction of rental equipment costs—Find hours saved by comparing new method to old. Actual rental rates are used in arriving at the dollar figure.

Record date idea went into effect.

If Suggestion is unacceptable, give logical reason why.

If idea is accepted, provide a brief summary of it to facilitate Committee and Board member review. To prevent misunderstanding, the investigator should restate in his or her own words on the evaluation sheet the suggested ideas, and the disposition write-ups should contain a direct statement on why the suggester's idea is accepted.

If results of putting an acceptable idea into effect fall into the "intangible" category—that is, the exact cost of the two methods cannot be determined or the savings are not easily measured or possible to measure—give award recommendation and reason for it. *Do not use the intangible award* if the results of the suggested change can be measured. An intangible award will be considered accomplished and installed when the change has been initiated through revised documentation or initiated procedure.

Provide information needed for Subcommittee and Board of Judges review, including:

- Certification that idea is in use and the effective date of installation.

- Comparison of old and new methods, listing all savings factors. If intangible, give award recommendation.

- If idea is unacceptable for use, give logical reason why. Suggester must be made to feel the idea has been carefully considered and any merits realized.

6.0 Awards

6.1 Basic Award

The basic award subject to the maximum set out in Section 6.2 is one sixth of the *gross* savings realized from the first year's application of an accepted idea. The gross award may range from $5 up to a maximum of $5000. Awards are considered as salary and are subject to withholding.

6.2 Maximum Award

The maximum award that will be awarded by the Board of Judges for any application of a Suggestion is $5000. Unless savings to justify the full award have already been realized, an initial award of $2000 is paid upon acceptance of the Suggestion, and the balance is paid on recalculation after the idea has been in use one full year. There is no interest paid on the "deferred balance."

6.3 Minimum Award

The minimum award is $5 per Suggestion and is authorized for any application of a Suggestion in which the calculated award would be $5 or less. Do not use the word *minimum* award in recommendation.

6.4 Intangible Award

An intangible award is recommended when savings cannot be calculated. It is either a $5 award for documentation corrections or ideas of convenience that tend to improve working conditions and/or employee morale or a $20 award for ideas where savings logic exists but the savings are difficult to quantify.

6.5 Safety Award

A $20 safety award is recommended for accepted safety suggestions.

6.6 Split Award/Joint Contributors/Team Suggestion/Quality Circles

A split award is the division of an award among two or more employees who submit an accepted Suggestion jointly or individually on the same date. The amount is calculated as a single award and divided equally among the eligible recipients. In the case of a Team Suggestion, the award is shared equally by eligible, nonexempt Team members involved in the submission. Exempt Team members will be given a $10 recognition award. "Team" awards are limited to safety and tangible awards only.

6.7 Action Award

An action award is made when the Suggestion motivates the solution of a problem that is not the solution proposed by the suggester. An action award is valued at 50 percent of the basic award, or one-twelfth of the first year's savings from the improved idea.

When the suggester's idea could have saved $600 (resulting in an award of $100), but a different solution is used saving $900, on which an action award would be $75, the suggester is entitled to the greater sum.

As a rule of thumb:

- A *full award* is paid when the employee Suggestion is workable, although it may be modified or improved by Engineering to increase savings.

- An action award is paid when the original employee Suggestion is not workable, but Engineering, as an outgrowth of the Suggestion at the time of the investigation, develops a *drastically different solution* to solve the same problem.

6.8 Reapplication Ideas

Reapplication ideas—that is, new and specific applications of an existing method—are paid the full award (one-sixth of a year's savings).

6.9 Buying a Principle

In "buying a principle," the award is for results that are part tangible and part intangible and is in full payment for all *known* or *anticipated* future applications of the principle. If, however, after the idea has been communicated to its areas of use and they have had the opportunity to put it in use (15 to 90 days), the suggester calls attention to an unforeseen or overlooked application possibility, he or she is eligible for an award based on that specific application.

6.10 Duplicate Ideas

If a Suggestion that duplicates an earlier, rejected one actually brings about corrective action, a full award is paid to the original suggester (provided it is within the two-year time limit), and an action award (50 percent) goes to the second suggester.

6.11 Former Employees and Retirees

If an employee should leave the Company before an award is approved, payment is still made upon approval of an idea in the same manner as if the suggester were still an employee.

7.0 Reasons for Nonacceptance

An employee who submits a Suggestion is entitled to a full and logical explanation of why an idea is not acceptable. As a guide to evaluating an idea and providing an explanation of nonacceptance, the following paragraphs list a number of reasons why a Suggestion might be rejected:

- The idea is not economically feasible under present conditions—that is, schedule limitations, excessive cost of installation, or space problems.

- A duplicate prior Suggestion is under active consideration.

- The idea is currently being implemented or evaluated.

- The idea is vague or incomplete and requires further explanation.

- The subject matter is ineligible—for example, contrary to Company policy or customer or government requirements.

- The subject matter falls within the scope of the suggester's job assignment. An employee under direct assignment to correct a problem is not eligible for an award for suggesting a solution to that problem.
- The idea does not solve the problem posed, or the problem does not exist.
- The Suggestion creates a new problem.
- The idea does not eliminate a hazard.
- The submittal is a complaint—not a Suggestion.
- The procedure suggested is considered general "shop practice."
- The Suggestion corrects an obvious typographical error on some form of documentation.
- The Suggestion involves routine maintenance/general repair, painting, heating, worn tools, illegible paperwork, and so on.
- The Suggestion concerns jobs set up on a temporary basis.

8.0 Company Rights

Company rights involved in the Suggestion System are:

- The Company reserves the right at any time without notice to terminate, amend, or extend the Suggestion System.
- The Company assumes no legal responsibility beyond the maximum award for any suggestion.
- The employee assigns all rights to the Company, including patents.
- The employee has the right to appeal, but the reviewed action of the Board of Judges or Subcommittee, depending on the size of the award, is final.

9.0 Processing the Suggestion

The following are the steps and procedures to be used by each individual involved in preparing or processing a Suggestion form.

Originator

- Prepare Suggestion following directions printed on the back of form.
- Submit the four-part form with Suggestion to immediate Supervisor.

Supervisor

- Thank the originator.

- Verify that employee has signed statement of acknowledgment of Terms/Rules of the Suggestion System.

- Read the Suggestion.

- Sign the Suggestion form and complete needed details.

- Determine if the nature and scope of the requested action is within your area of decision authority. If it is, analyze Suggestion recommendation and take appropriate action to implement or reject. Communicate with suggester where possible.

- If the requested action is not within your area of decision, forward completed form to proper investigating department. (The "appropriate investigator" is one who is in a position to evaluate the idea and, if acceptable, put it into effect.) If you are not sure, check by telephone with person you choose.

- Distribute four copies: Remove and forward the SUGGESTION SYSTEM copy immediately to the Suggestion Administrator and EMPLOYEE'S copy to suggester; file SUPERVISOR'S copy. ACTION copy to evaluator.

- Be impersonal during investigation and evaluation.

Note: Employee supervisor has the responsibility for follow-up on the investigation of suggestions for his or her employees.

Suggestion System Administrator

- Date SUGGESTION SYSTEM copy; complete data processing; and when returned, place in tickler file.

Person Possessing Decision Authority
    If idea is acceptable:

- Enter a clear explanation of the decision in the space headed "Disposition." Sign and date.

- Perform (or cause to be performed) the required action to implement the idea. For example:

Write Tool Order
Write Maintenance Work Order
Change Process Sheet(s)
Write Purchase Requisition
Write Memorandum and so on.

- After idea is installed, calculate savings and obtain IE (Industrial Engineering) verification.

- Return Suggestion to employee's Supervisor (not applicable if Supervisor accomplishes the disposition action).

If idea is not acceptable:

- Enter reason for not accepting in the space headed "Disposition."
- Return Suggestion to employee's Supervisor.

Supervisor

- Notify originator of action taken. If Suggestion is accepted, tell how his or her recommendation is being implemented. *Do not discuss any estimated potential savings or calculations prior to Suggestion System Committee action.* If not accepted, explain reason. Send both accepted and unapproved Suggestions back to the Suggestion System Administrator.

Suggestion Administrator

- Take approved Suggestions to the Subcommittees where they are accepted, rejected, returned for further information, or passed on to the Board of Judges.
- Notify management of awards of $100 or more for suitable publicity arrangements.
- File original Suggestion and keep for seven years from final decision date.

NOMINAL GROUP TECHNIQUE

Nominal group technique (NGT) is a group problem-solving process. It is a structured form of brainstorming that has some special features.

- The process causes all of the group to be part of the discussion and decisions.

- Everyone in the group is equal from the standpoint of sharing ideas.

- The process keeps dominant personalities in check.

- The results have a high chance of being successful.

NGT is a problem-solving process that works with task teams or quality circles. It is a powerful tool in almost any meeting. NGT is not a replacement for circles or teams, but rather a tool to lead them to making better decisions.

The process can be used two ways.

1. An NGT meeting can be called to resolve a problem prestated to the group. In this case, it is necessary to ensure that the group understands the task statement and that any needed modifications

191

are made before the meeting starts. The group is selected to include all of the ideas from workers in the various jobs involved in the task being analyzed. A good solution requires the input of all parties involved.

2. NGT can be used as the basic process for ongoing problem-solving teams. The team would use NGT as a method of identifying a range of problems that need investigation and prioritize the order on which they would be worked. The team would establish the task statement and usually wait until the next meeting for NGT analysis.

In both cases, it is best to let the group or team have several days to gather data relevant to the problem identified in the task statement. With some preparation, the results of NGT will be better than those without preparation.

It may be necessary to direct some data collection as a part of the meeting notice or after the voting in the first meeting. There is no reason that the decision must be made in the first meeting. Frequently there is the need for added data or the addition of other people that could bring a new perspective to the group.

LEADING A NOMINAL GROUP PROCESS

Group members

- Seven people are optimum.
- All aspects of the task should be represented.
- All should be experienced in the task involved.

Preparations

- A meeting notice should be distributed at least one week ahead of time stating the task to be discussed, the time, place, and any special instructions to group members.
- A meeting room large enough to accommodate the group comfortably should be reserved.
- The table and chairs should be arranged in a *U* with the flip chart in the middle or at the open end.

Supplies

- Flip chart and paper, marking pens, voting cards, masking tape, tablet paper, and pencils are all needed.

Facilitator

- Knows the NGT process

• Assures that the group follows the process

- Maintains control of the group

- Creates an open and cooperative atmosphere

The facilitator opens the meeting by welcoming everyone in the group. If the group contains strangers, identify each person by name, work area, and any data related to the task. A sign-up sheet should be circulated to get the correct spelling of names and other pertinent information. The task statement is reviewed to be sure that all of the participants understand and agree with the content.

The facilitator reviews the rules of NGT.

1. During round-robin recording all ideas are accepted without challenge or comments. Clarification is done later.

2. Everyone should try to gain added ideas from other members' ideas. This is called piggybacking.

3. Clarification of ideas must come from the originator. The facilitator must prevent any ridicule of ideas.

4. All voting must be done in secret. The facilitator must prevent any pressures to control voting.

THE SIX STEPS FOR NOMINAL GROUP TECHNIQUE

1. **Task Statement**—The task statement should be open-ended. This means that there is not a limit on the scope of the task and a solution is not preselected. A task statement may be determined by the group from a listing of processes or products that the group feels could be improved for the benefit of the organization. The task statement must have approval by the group.

2. **Silent Generation**—Using the tablet paper provided, each group member spends five to 10 minutes identifying his or her answer to the task statement. There is to be no discussion during this time except to clarify the task statement.

   The time allotted is specified before the group starts. The facilitator maintains silence and encourages those who finish early not to disturb others. If everyone in the group is done, the facilitator may move to the next step.

   The facilitator can take part as an equal voting member or act as a professional resource to the group.

3. **Round-Robin Recording**—Either the facilitator or a volunteer recorder will write down one idea from each group member in turn. The order of participation is strictly followed and only one idea per turn is accepted. The recording is done on the flip chart and the

group member is asked if his or her idea is properly recorded. If it is necessary to shorten many of the idea statements, this must be done with the approval of the source.

Do not force anyone to be a recorder. There is a threat of spelling competence and the risk of looking foolish. Also, some people will not willingly take on a recording task for a variety of reasons. It may be best for the facilitator to act as recorder.

It is permissible to say "pass" at any time and reenter the idea input at the next round. The facilitator should encourage group members to piggyback by finding new ideas from the ideas of others in the group. The process should not be threatening; it should be encouraging and fun. When all group members say "pass," the facilitator closes recording.

4. **Clarification**—The recorder should first identify each idea with a letter (or number) to simplify reference to the idea.

The facilitator should lead an open discussion to clarify each of the ideas and to combine them into fewer ideas where possible. The clarification should not become a vote-promoting process. The person who originated the idea should not be placed in a role of defending his or her idea.

If the flip charts are messed up, the remaining ideas should be transferred to a new page prior to voting. If possible, leave space ahead of each idea for the identifying letter and behind for the voting results. If the data are copied, hang the old charts on the wall so everyone is sure that no ideas were lost.

5. **Voting and Ranking**—The facilitator has everyone review the combined ideas and vote for the three they think are the most important. Voting is to be done as a secret process using cards or similar paper. Voting gives 5 points for the first choice, 3 points for the second choice, and 1 point for the third choice. These voting values help spread out the results and provides more accurate data.

Each person completes his or her voting cards and turns them in to the facilitator or designated person. The facilitator assigns one or two of the group to read off the vote data so the results can be tallied on the flip chart.

Obtaining secret written votes eliminates any social pressures. Having one of the group call out the data prevents the voting from being controlled by the leader. The posting of the ranking on the flip chart displays the results of all of the voting and generates consensus or ownership of the results. The mathematical process of voting and summing the votes increases the accuracy over a show-of-hands process.

If the voting is close and there are a large number of ideas with similar total ranking, it may be necessary to repeat the voting using only those with high scores. This will allow the group to focus on fewer ideas and rate them accordingly.

A preprinted voting card is suggested rather than using blank 3-by 5-inch cards. The use of preprinted cards adds to the seriousness of the process and also helps maintain anonymity.

6. **Discussion of Results**—The output of NGT is a list of ideas that covers a wide range of possibilities related to the original task statement. These ideas frequently need more data or inputs from added persons to the group before the best response to the task statement can be selected.

If all the needed data and persons with vital inputs are present, then a final selection can be made with commitment by the entire group.

NGT will produce results that are accepted by the entire group and reflect the dynamics of group thinking. The structure of NGT carefully builds the acceptance of the process and the results.

IDEA VOTING CARD

Idea Letter

Item or Idea

_____

_____

_____

	Priority Ranking
5—Highest 1—Lowest	

PROCESS
SUMMARY CHARTS

Cause-and-Effect Diagrams with Cards (CEDAC):
A Tool for Problem Solving in a Group Environment

Cause-and-effect diagrams with cards (CEDAC® Productivity Inc.) are graphic tools that are very effective tools for use in problem analysis. The process utilizes both management expertise and worker know-how in solving problems. It brings the improvement process out of the supervisor's office and onto the factory floor.

What is it?

Step-by-step group process for problem solving
• Identifies facts
• Proposes solutions
• Tests solutions
• Documents effect on problem
• Uses participative approach, group consensus

Why use it?

Because it works.
• Makes problem visible
• Sets target and improvement measure
• Focuses on problem, instead of people
• Builds accurate and factual record of improvements.
• Continues to work, overtime, to further reduce problems and improve the process

Step 1

Develop an effect statement.
Write statement that describes and quantifies problem effect. Use numerical and historical data. Make statement visible on CEDAC diagram.

Step 2

Determine an improvement measure.
Decide on how to measure results of improvements, what data best measure results, how we get the data, and how often we measure. (The more the better.)

Step 3

Determine a target. Develop a target statement.
• Target must be based on improvement measure. Target must have a date. (The sooner the better.)
• Make it visual. Complete effect (right) side of CEDAC diagram. At a minimum this should include the following:
  – Problem effect statement
  – Problem improvement measure
  – Target effect statement
  – Project leader
  – Project start date
  – Target completion date

Step 4

Generate fact-finding cards and post on diagram.
Facts about the problem are written on small colored cards. Avoid attempting to solve problems here. Just get the facts as you know them. Measurable facts are better than beliefs, but all are accepted. Facts go on left side of fishbone.

Step 5

Generate improvement cards and post on diagram.
Improvement ideas are on different colored cards and posted on the opposite (right) side of fishbone. All improvement ideas are accepted, but they must be written on improvement cards. Synthesize similar cards as needed and categorize them on major trunks of diagram.

Step 6

Select and test improvement ideas.
Members review and evaluate improvement ideas. Try to get consensus on ideas to test. Members mark cards with a dot to signify their acceptance. Manager still retains final authority for test and installation. Try only one idea at a time. Post results of improvement, either good or bad.

Step 7

Incorporate successful improvement ideas.
Display improvement card for recognition. Repeat steps 3 through 6 until target is reached.

Design of Experiments:
A Tool for Product or Process Problem Solving

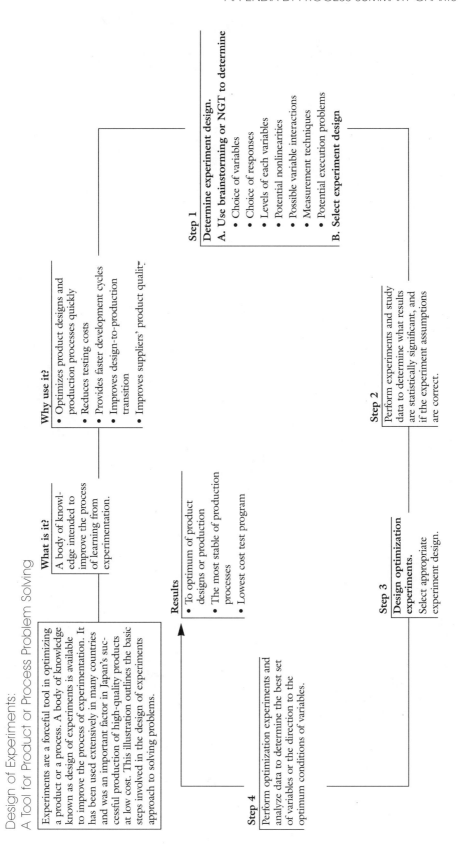

Experiments are a forceful tool in optimizing a product or a process. A body of knowledge known as design of experiments is available to improve the process of experimentation. It has been used extensively in many countries and was an important factor in Japan's successful production of high-quality products at low cost. This illustration outlines the basic steps involved in the design of experiments approach to solving problems.

What is it?

A body of knowledge intended to improve the process of learning from experimentation.

Why use it?

- Optimizes product designs and production processes quickly
- Reduces testing costs
- Provides faster development cycles
- Improves design-to-production transition
- Improves suppliers' product quality

Results

- To optimum of product designs or production
- The most stable of production processes
- Lowest cost test program

Step 1

Determine experiment design.

A. Use brainstorming or NGT to determine

- Choice of variables
- Choice of responses
- Levels of each variables
- Potential nonlinearities
- Possible variable interactions
- Measurement techniques
- Potential execution problems

B. Select experiment design

Step 2

Perform experiments and study data to determine what results are statistically significant, and if the experiment assumptions are correct.

Step 3

Design optimization experiments.

Select appropriate experiment design.

Step 4

Perform optimization experiments and analyze data to determine the best set of variables or the direction to the optimum conditions of variables.

Ergonomics (Human Factors Engineering):
A Tool for Achieving Improvement in the Workplace

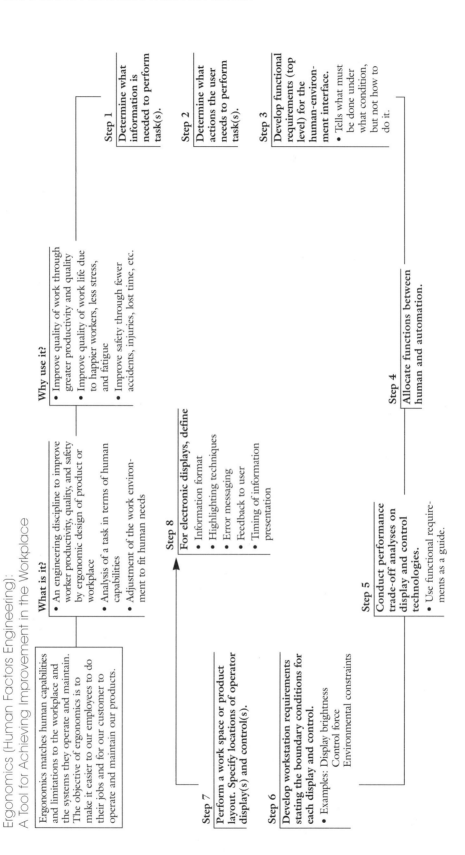

Ergonomics matches human capabilities and limitations to the workplace and the systems they operate and maintain. The objective of ergonomics is to make it easier to our employees to do their jobs and for our customer to operate and maintain our products.

What is it?
- An engineering discipline to improve worker productivity, quality, and safety by ergonomic design of product or workplace
- Analysis of a task in terms of human capabilities
- Adjustment of the work environment to fit human needs

Why use it?
- Improve quality of work through greater productivity and quality
- Improve quality of work life due to happier workers, less stress, and fatigue
- Improve safety through fewer accidents, injuries, lost time, etc.

Step 1
Determine what information is needed to perform task(s).

Step 2
Determine what actions the user needs to perform task(s).

Step 3
Develop functional requirements (top level) for the human-environment interface.
- Tells what must be done under what condition, but not how to do it.

Step 4
Allocate functions between human and automation.

Step 5
Conduct performance trade-off analyses on display and control technologies.
- Use functional requirements as a guide.

Step 6
Develop workstation requirements stating the boundary conditions for each display and control.
- Examples: Display brightness
  Control force
  Environmental constraints

Step 7
Perform a work space or product layout. Specify locations of operator display(s) and control(s).

Step 8
For electronic displays, define
- Information format
- Highlighting techniques
- Error messaging
- Feedback to user
- Timing of information presentation

Input/Output Analysis:
A Tool for Improving the Definition of Roles, Responsibilities, and Interdependencies

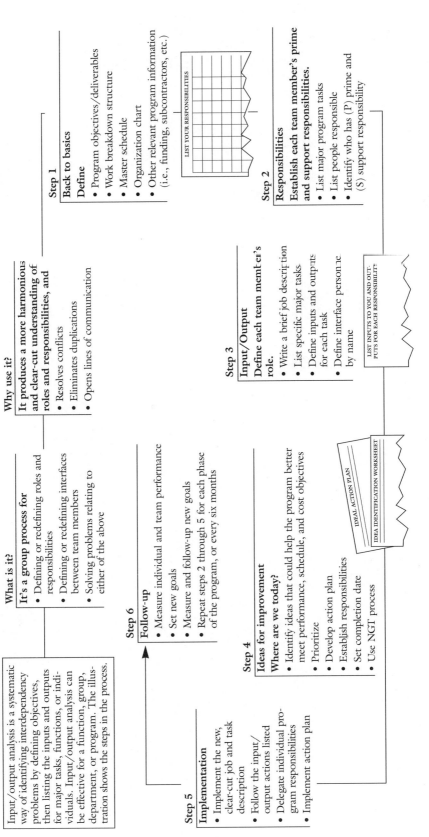

Input/output analysis is a systematic way of identifying interdependency problems by defining objectives, then listing the inputs and outputs for major tasks, functions, or individuals. Input/output analysis can be effective for a function, group, department, or program. The illustration shows the steps in the process.

What is it?

It's a group process for

- Defining or redefining roles and responsibilities
- Defining or redefining interfaces between team members
- Solving problems relating to either of the above

Why use it?

It produces a more harmonious and clear-cut understanding of roles and responsibilities, and

- Resolves conflicts
- Eliminates duplications
- Opens lines of communication

Step 1
Back to basics
Define
- Program objectives/deliverables
- Work breakdown structure
- Master schedule
- Organization chart
- Other relevant program information (i.e., funding, subcontractors, etc.)

LIST YOUR RESPONSIBILITIES

Step 2
Responsibilities
Establish each team member's prime and support responsibilities.
- List major program tasks
- List people responsible
- Identify who has (P) prime and (S) support responsibility

Step 3
Input/Output
Define each team member's role.
- Write a brief job description
- List specific major tasks
- Define inputs and outputs for each task
- Define interface person by name

LIST INPUTS TO YOU AND OUTPUTS FOR EACH RESPONSIBILITY

Step 4
Ideas for improvement
Where are we today?
- Identify ideas that could help the program better meet performance, schedule, and cost objectives
- Prioritize
- Develop action plan
- Establish responsibilities
- Set completion date
- Use NGT process

IDEAL ACTION PLAN

IDEA IDENTIFICATION WORKSHEET

Step 5
Implementation
- Implement the new, clear-cut job and task description
- Follow the input/output actions listed
- Delegate individual program responsibilities
- Implement action plan

Step 6
Follow-up
- Measure individual and team performance
- Set new goals
- Measure and follow-up new goals
- Repeat steps 2 through 5 for each phase of the program, or every six months

Just-in-Time (JIT):
A Pull Rather than a Push Manufacturing Control System

Just-in-time (JIT) is a pull-type manufacturing control system that provides
• The right material
• At the right place
• At the right time
The system emphasizes problem solving and utilizes employee involvement and group process techniques

What is it?
It is a pull-type manufacturing process that involves
• Enforced problem solving
• "Right the first time" philosophy
• Pull rather than push system
• Linear scheduling

Why use it?
The JIT system forces waste elimination by
• Requiring a higher quality product
• Reducing lot size and inventories
• Reducing set-up times
Note: JIT is a form of process cycle time reduction and can be applied to processes other than manufacturing.

Step 1
Establish the team/goal/vision.
• Establish team of supervisors operators, and engineers.
• Establish culture of do-it-once, do-it-right. Shut line down if something is not right.
• Establish goals/vision.
 – Material is either moving between operation or is having value added.
 – Zero defects is a realizable goal.
 – Rework, scrap, inspection, stocking, setup, and inventories are all waste to be eliminated.

Step 2
Define the process flow.
• Develop a flowchart
• Estimate process cycle time
• Balance line with staff/facilities
• Use a team approach

Step 3
Identify yields and improvement action.
• Identify yield of each step in process
• Use Pareto technique to determine which step to fix first
• Implement continuous improvement actions to improve yields

Step 4
Install a linear scheduling system.
• Must accomplish the same amount from each operation/shift
• Self-scheduling visually obvious

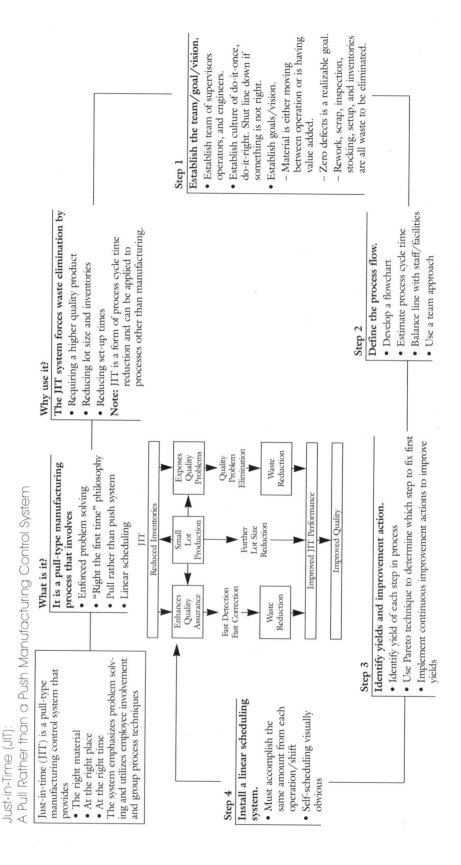

Nominal Group Technique (NGT)/Brainstorming:
A Tool for Idea Generation and Problem Solving

Using nominal group technique (NGT), a group of employees (workers, supervisors, managers) work together to identify problem areas. Everyone participates in this process, which isolates specific problems quickly. The illustration shows the process in detail.

What is it?

It's a group process for identifying
- Ideas
- Issues
- Solutions
- Problems

It's a proactive search process.

All participants contribute equally.

Why use it?

It produces many ideas/solutions in a short time.

It focuses on problems, not people, and opens the lines of communication within a group.

It ensures participation.

It tolerates conflicting ideas.

It captures creative ideas.

Ground Rules

1. Do not judge or editorialize.
2. Allow no members to judge or editorialize.
3. Stay with "round-robin" turns so no one is missed.
4. Do not overlook shy people or let aggressive/informal leaders dominate.
5. Instruct people to make own decisions about redundant ideas. If someone calls out an idea on a participant's list, that participant should cross it off his or her list. If the thought is significantly different and merits consideration, the participant should call it out on a turn. It is the participant's decision to make.

Step 1

The NGT process in action

Group leader addresses subject, presents the problem/issue to be dealt with by the group, and gives instructions.

Step 2

Idea generation and silent writing
- Participants seated at tables
- Participants have paper and pencil
- Participants write out whatever ideas "pop" into their heads
- 10 to 15 minutes for writing
- Leader has flip chart
- Leader may participate

Step 3

Idea gathering; leader conducts "round-robin"
- Each person contributes an idea in turn
- Leader may participate in turn
- Ideas written on flip chart
- All ideas written as stated
- Post all filled pages for all to view
- Continue until each person passes
- Participants may delete ideas from list
- Participants may add ideas
- No evaluation/judgment by leader or participant
- Review complete list for priority ranking

At this point leader may restate general issue or problem under consideration.

Step 4

Process/clarify ideas
- Each item discussed
- Some combined, new ideas added
- Every participant understands ideas

Step 5

Priority setting

Participants silently examine clarified items
- Participants silently select their top 3, 5, or 7 (about 20 to 25% of list)
- Participants call out their top priority items
- Record tally on flip chart

Step 6

Action plan
- Review top five priority items
- Develop consensus on who will develop action
- Set completion date for plan

203

Statistical Process Control (SPC):
A Tool for Solving Problems and Improving Performance

SPC methods provide a disciplined means of identifying and solving problems, and can be utilized by all people whether they are production, engineering, or administrative. The methods are especially useful when the process involves people from multiple departments, as they provide a framework for the people to use in determining and making improvements. The diagram shows the steps involved in the process.

What is it?
- A disciplined way of identifying and problems and improving performance
- The statistical measurement of process variations
- An accurate and timely visual representation of status

Why use it?
- Serves as an effective tool for improving performance
- Identifies problems quickly and accurately
- Provides quantifiable data for analysis
- Provides better understanding of process and how it works
- Encourages participative process with decisions made by people doing job.

Step 1
Identifying problems or performance improvement areas;
(Conducting capability study to determine if process is capable of producing desired result)
- NGT

Step 2
Formulating the problem in writing
- Better understanding

Step 3
Identifying possible problem causes or potential
- Cause-and-effect analysis

Step 4
Collecting data
- Existing data
- New data

Step 5
Organizing the data
- Graphs
- Charts
- Diagrams
- Pareto charts
- Histograms

Step 6
Applying statistical techniques
- Control charts

Step 7
Analyzing results
- Determining variations

Step 8
Taking corrective action
- Changing the process

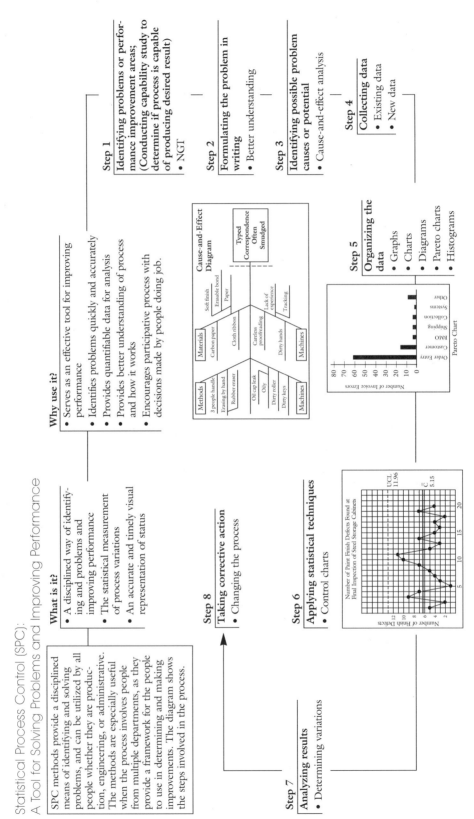

Cause-and-Effect Diagram

Materials
- Soft finish
- Erasable bond
- Carbon paper
- Paper
- Cloth ribbon

Methods
- 3 people handle
- Erasing by hand
- Rubber eraser

Typed Correspondence Often Smudged

- Careless proofreading
- Lack of experience
- Tracking
- Oil cap leak
- Oily
- Dirty roller
- Dirty keys
- Dirty hands

Machines

Machines

Pareto Chart

Number of Invoice Errors

Order Entry, Customer, BMO, Shipping, Collection, Systems, Other

Number of Paint Finish Defects Found at Final Inspection of Steel Storage Cabinets

Number of Finish Defects

UCL 11.96
C 5.15

Team Building:
A Tool for Improving Team Performance

A team is a group of people working together for a common goal when accomplishment of that goal requires interdependence. In organizations it is often the case that to get the job done we need to work together as a team.
Because of this need to work in a team atmosphere, leaders and managers need to work on the development and maintenance of the team—this is called team building. Members of teams look to the leader to provide them help working in the team environment. Team building is a regular part of any team leader's job. As you develop your work plan, plan time for team-building activities. It may head off schedule problems, cost products, misunderstandings, and confusion later on. It is a good investment of your time as a manager or team leader.

What is it?
Team building is the process of developing and maintaining a group of people who are working together for a common goal.

Why use it?
Often the accomplishment of a goal requires interdependence. To get the job done we need to work together as a team.

Ground Rules
1. Don't ignore team/team member problems. Think through the symptoms and uncover the cause(s). Focus on the problem not on personalities.
2. Maintain a balance between the needs of the individuals, the team, and the goal.

The Process in Action
Step 1
Identify the team.
The team ideally should be made up of people who share a common goal, which requires an interdependence.

Step 2
Develop the team.
• Develop and maintain trust, respect, and dignity for all members.
• Locate people in the same area if possible.
• Develop a team identity (a logo, team name, etc.).
• Set aside a social time so team members can get to know each other.
• Discuss how members are or are not working together in an open and nonthreatening way.

Step 3
Identify the team goals.
• Goals should be set in a participative manner as much as possible. The NGT process can be used.
• The team goals and priorities must be understood and accepted by the members.
• Ensure that members are clear in what their contributions are and with whom they need to interface.

Step 4
Recognize team accomplishments regularly, publically, and privately. Teams, like individuals, want to do a good job and need to feel that their contributions are important.

Step 5
Maintain the team.
Teams are a living entity and thus change with time. In order for a team to continue to be successful it must recognize and cope with change. To do this, repeat steps 2, 3, and 4 as necessary.

205

Value Analysis (VE/VA Value Engineering/Value Analysis):
A Tool for Improving Processes and Products

Value analysis is a structured system to investigate how each part of a product or process contributes to the operation of the system or the performance of the product. The process then leads the V/A team through evaluating alternate solutions and selecting the solution offering the best result. This process is widely used in America, Europe, and Japan.

What is it?

V/A is a participative group process that optimizes evaluation of a product or a process.

Why use V/A?
- Provides excellent insight into possible variables or changes
- Optimizes choice of process or product
- Concentrates on the function, not the item

Step 1

Select a project where
- Product or process needs reduction of costs
- Project has a two- to three-year future
- Forecasts for use are known
- Documentation and cost data are available
- Potential for saving warrants study investment
- Team advisory support is available
- Management support is available
- Supporting materials are available (forms, materials, products, etc.)

Step 2

Select a team.
- 4 to 7 members
- Key expertise on the team
- Representation of all involved groups
- Members available for 2-1/2 weeks of half days
- A balance of members with and without project experience

Step 3

Information phase
1. What is it (the project).
2. What function must it perform?
3. What function does it perform?
4. What does each function cost?
(Use a two-word verb/noun description for items 2 and 3. Example: An automobile TRANSPORTS PEOPLE.)

Step 4

Creativity phase
Find what else will perform each function.
Use as appropriate
- Brainstorming
- Attribute listings
- Morphological analysis
- Synectics
- Input/output analysis
- Gordon technique
- Hypothetical situations
- Nominal group technique

Step 5

Planning
- Evaluate brainstorming
- Put $ value on each idea
- Establish alternate plans
- Assign data gathering
- Set a date for review

Step 6

Execution phase
- Evaluate alternatives
- Assess risks
- Identify organizational roadblocks
- Test and evaluate the solution or solutions

Step 7

Reporting
- Present benefits of the plan
- Answer questions
- Support implementation

Step 8

Re-do the process
- Evaluate the process for a complete new analysis

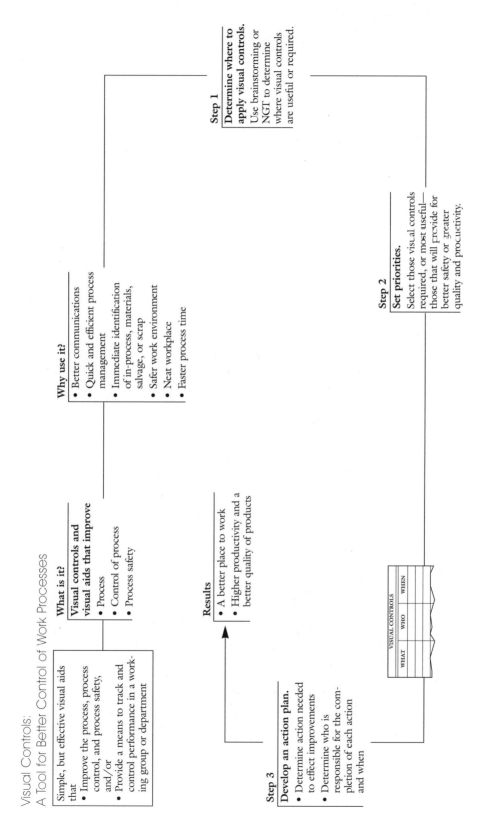

Visual Controls:
A Tool for Better Control of Work Processes

Simple, but effective visual aids that
• Improve the process, process control, and process safety, and/or
• Provide a means to track and control process performance in a working group or department

What is it?
Visual controls and visual aids that improve
• Process
• Control of process
• Process safety

Why use it?
• Better communications
• Quick and efficient process management
• Immediate identification of in-process, materials, salvage, or scrap
• Safer work environment
• Neat workplace
• Faster process time

Results
• A better place to work
• Higher productivity and a better quality of products

Step 1
Determine where to apply visual controls.
Use brainstorming or NGT to determine where visual controls are useful or required.

Step 2
Set priorities.
Select those visual controls required, or most useful—those that will provide for better safety or greater quality and productivity.

Step 3
Develop an action plan.
• Determine action needed to effect improvements
• Determine who is responsible for the completion of each action and when

VISUAL CONTROLS		
WHAT	WHO	WHEN

Work Flow Analysis (WFA):
A Tool for Achieving Improvement in Processes

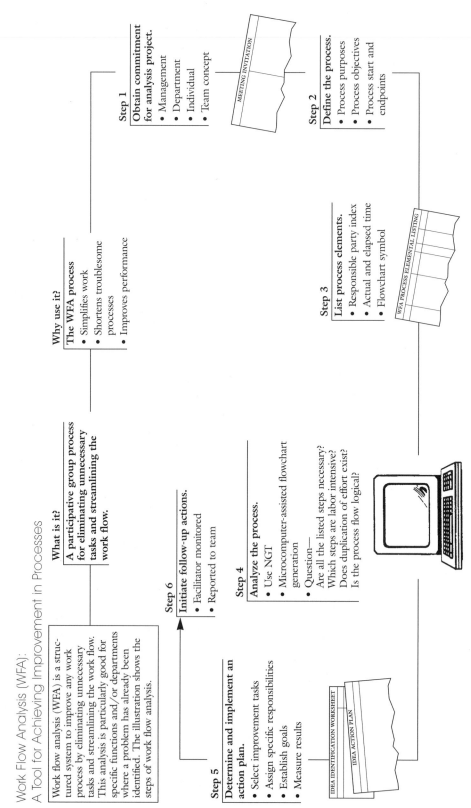

What is it?

A participative group process for eliminating unnecessary tasks and streamlining the work flow.

Work flow analysis (WFA) is a structured system to improve any work process by eliminating unnecessary tasks and streamlining the work flow. This analysis is particularly good for specific functions and/or departments where a problem has already been identified. The illustration shows the steps of work flow analysis.

Why use it?

The WFA process
- Simplifies work
- Shortens troublesome processes
- Improves performance

Step 1
Obtain commitment for analysis project.
- Management
- Department
- Individual
- Team concept

MEETING INVITATION

Step 2
Define the process.
- Process purposes
- Process objectives
- Process start and endpoints

Step 3
List process elements.
- Responsible party index
- Actual and elapsed time
- Flowchart symbol

WFA PROCESS ELEMENTAL LISTING

Step 4
Analyze the process.
- Use NGT
- Microcomputer-assisted flowchart generation
- Question—
  Are all the listed steps necessary?
  Which steps are labor intensive?
  Does duplication of effort exist?
  Is the process flow logical?

Step 5
Determine and implement an action plan.
- Select improvement tasks
- Assign specific responsibilities
- Establish goals
- Measure results

IDEA IDENTIFICATION WORKSHEET
IDEA ACTION PLAN

Step 6
Initiate follow-up actions.
- Facilitator monitored
- Reported to team

MEASURING PERFORMANCE

How are we doing? Did we meet our plan? How much have we improved? To determine the answers to these questions and others, we need to use measurements as yardsticks. With comparisons of past, present, and projected performance, we can measure our changes.

More importantly, measurements show us where to take action, and they evaluate the actions already taken. They give us the information we need to

- Determine progress against plans, goals, and needs.

- Identify problems or changes as they occur so corrective action can be taken.

- Evaluate the extent and effectiveness of changes and improvements.

- Motivate people and increase job satisfaction. People pay more attention to measurements when progress can then be seen and felt.

- Determine and evaluate trends.

Although measurements are effective aids to performance improvement, they are not infallible. The best measurements do not attempt too much or claim too much. It's the people who solve problems, not the measurements. But the right measurements can tell people where to apply their problem-solving skills.

TYPES OF MEASUREMENTS

To determine progress, different types of measurements must be conducted at different levels of the organization. In all cases, improvement is the objective of measurement, not measurement for its own sake.

Measurements can be broken down into two basic categories—macromeasurements and micromeasurements.

Macromeasurements

Macromeasurements are used at the divisional, operational, and functional levels, and are capable of being added to give totals. These totals indicate performance trends and, while not giving the reasons for changes, show where further analysis is needed. The totals cannot be used to compare operations or divisions since the nature of their business dictates that there will be differences. If a division's trend varies greatly from the others, however, the macromeasurement will suggest a closer look to determine the cause.

Micromeasurements

Micromeasurements are done at the department or work group level to improve productivity and quality of work. These measurements must be developed, agreed upon, and used as a diagnostic tool by the people actually doing the work. Measurement without ownership is worse than no measurement at all.

To be effective, micromeasurements must have the following characteristics:

- They must be developed and followed by the people doing the work being measured.

- They must be periodic to indicate changes as they occur.

- They must be applied to groups or processes.

- Their results must be analyzed by those who can influence and are responsible for those results.

- They may consist of a family of related measurements with understood limitations. This is more useful than trying to find one all-inclusive measurement.

EXAMPLES OF MICROMEASUREMENTS BY FUNCTION

Production

$$\frac{\text{Direct Hours}}{\textit{Standard Hours}}$$

$$\frac{\text{Earned Hours}}{\textit{Direct Hours}}$$

$$\frac{\text{Indirect Hours}}{\textit{Direct Hours}}$$

$$\frac{\text{Salvage Hours}}{\textit{Direct Hours}}$$

$$\frac{\text{Setup Hours}}{\textit{Earned Hours}}$$

$$\frac{\text{Direct Labor \$}}{\textit{Standard Hours}}$$

$$\frac{\text{\# Units Accepted}}{\textit{\# Units Inspected}}$$

$$\frac{\text{Wait Time Hours}}{\textit{Direct Labor Hours}}$$

$$\frac{\text{Units Scheduled}}{\textit{Units Produced}}$$

$$\frac{\text{Complete Kits Issued}}{\textit{Total Kits Issued}}$$

$$\frac{\text{Cost of Sales}}{\textit{Gross Inventory}}$$

$$\frac{\text{Scrap Costs}}{\textit{Labor Burden Material Additions}}$$

$$\frac{\text{Labor Burden Material and Support Costs}}{\textit{\# Units Produced}}$$

$$\frac{\text{Fixed Price Cost of Sales}}{\textit{Gross Net Inventory}}$$

$$\frac{\text{Sales/Value Added Sales}}{\textit{Direct Head Count}}$$

$$\frac{\text{Sales/Value Added Sales}}{\textit{Total Head Count}}$$

$$\frac{\text{Product Build and Support Hours}}{\textit{Equivalent Units}}$$

$$\frac{\text{Customer Accepted Lots}}{\textit{Lots Submitted}}$$

$$\frac{\text{Warranty Repair Costs}}{\textit{Sales}}$$

$$\frac{\text{Sales/Value Added Sales}}{\textit{Indirect Head Count}}$$

$$\frac{\text{Cost of Quality}}{\textit{Cost of Sales}}$$

$$\frac{\text{Profit Before Income Taxes}}{\textit{Employees}}$$

$$\frac{\text{Act. Process Cycle Time}}{\textit{Base Process Cycle Time}}$$

$$\frac{\text{Inventory Shortage}}{\textit{Inventory Additions}}$$

$$\frac{\text{Total Production Hours}}{\textit{Direct Earned Hours}}$$

$$\frac{\text{Delinquent Units x Selling Price}}{\textit{Average Daily Sales}}$$

$$\frac{\text{Production Support Costs}}{\textit{Production Labor Burden Material Costs}}$$

$$\frac{\text{Indirect Head Count}}{\textit{Direct Head Count}}$$

$$\frac{\text{Production Hourly Head Count}}{\textit{Production Control Head Count}}$$

$$\frac{\text{Production Hourly Head Count}}{\textit{Production Engineering Head Count}}$$

$$\frac{\text{\# Defects}}{\textit{\# Units Inspected}}$$

$$\frac{\text{Hours on Labor Ticket Rejects}}{\textit{Total Hours Reported}}$$

$$\frac{\text{Actual Burden Rate}}{\textit{Planned Burden Rate}}$$

$$\frac{\text{\# Personnel Transfers}}{\textit{Head Count}}$$

$$\frac{\text{Prod. Lines on Just in Time}}{\textit{Total Prod. Lines}}$$

EXAMPLES OF MICROMEASUREMENTS BY FUNCTION (continued)

Engineering

$$\frac{\text{\# Std. Parts in Releases}}{\textit{Total \# Parts in Releases}}$$

$$\frac{\text{Direct Labor}}{\textit{Total Time Reporting Labor}}$$

$$\frac{\text{Sales/Value Added Sales}}{\textit{Time Reporting Head Count}}$$

$$\frac{\text{Sales/Value Added Sales}}{\textit{Indirect Head Count}}$$

$$\frac{\text{Sales/Value Added Sales}}{\textit{Total Head Count}}$$

$$\frac{\text{\# Software Instructions}}{\textit{\# Software Engineers}}$$

$$\frac{\text{Cost to Prepare Drawings}}{\textit{\# Drawings Produced}}$$

$$\frac{\text{Prod. Build Hrs. on Layouts}}{\textit{Prod. Build Hrs.}}$$

$$\frac{\text{Profit Before Income Taxes}}{\textit{Employees}}$$

$$\frac{\text{Actual Burden Rate}}{\textit{Planned Burden Rate}}$$

$$\frac{\text{\# Personnel Transfer}}{\textit{Head Count}}$$

$$\frac{\text{Projected Unit Build Cost}}{\textit{Target Unit Build Cost}}$$

$$\frac{\text{Production Support Costs}}{\textit{Production Labor Burden Material Costs}}$$

$$\frac{\text{\# Engineering Change Orders}}{\textit{\# Drawings}}$$

$$\frac{\text{Hrs. on Rejected Time Reports}}{\textit{Total Hrs. Reported}}$$

$$\frac{\text{Projects with Plans}}{\textit{Total Projects}}$$

$$\frac{\text{Projects Overrun \$}}{\textit{Total Projects \$}}$$

$$\frac{\text{Computer-Aided Design Hours Usage}}{\textit{Computer-Aided Hours Available}}$$

Service Engineering

$$\frac{\text{\$ Orders Received YTD}}{\textit{\$ Orders Planned YTD}}$$

$$\frac{\text{\$ Order Received Month/Year}}{\textit{\# Marketers/Contract Admin.}}$$

$$\frac{\text{Total Operations Personnel}}{\textit{Service Engineering Personnel}}$$

$$\frac{\text{Sales/Value Added Sales}}{\textit{Service Engineering Head Count}}$$

$$\frac{\text{Operations Budget}}{\textit{Service Engineering Budget}}$$

$$\frac{\text{\$ Delinquent Deliveries}}{\textit{Average Daily Sales}}$$

$$\frac{\text{\# Proposals}}{\textit{\# Marketing Reps.}}$$

$$\frac{\text{\$ Orders Received}}{\textit{Service Engineering Budget}}$$

$$\frac{\text{\# Active Contracts}}{\textit{\# Contract Administrators}}$$

$$\frac{\text{Fixed Price Orders with Progress Payments}}{\textit{Total \# Fixed Price Orders}}$$

$$\frac{\text{Sales Proposal \$}}{\textit{\$ Orders Received}}$$

$$\frac{\text{Proposals Submitted}}{\textit{Proposals Won}}$$

$$\frac{\text{Service Engineering Budget}}{\textit{Operations Sales}}$$

EXAMPLES OF MICROMEASUREMENTS BY FUNCTION (continued)

Human Resources

Change Notices Processed
———————————————
 # Compensation Clericals

Sales/Value Added Sales
———————————————
*Employee Relations
Head Count*

Total Operations Head
Count
———————————————
*Employee Relations
Head Count*

Change Notice Errors
———————————————
Total Change Notices

People Interviewed
and Hired
———————————————
 # People Interviewed

Operations Support
———————————————
*Employee Relations
Budget*

Elapsed Time of
Unprocessed ECRs
———————————————
 # Unprocessed ECRs

Insurance Claims
Processed
———————————————
*# Insurance Claim
Clerks*

Lost Time for Injuries
———————————————
Total Hours Worked

Workers Compensation
Costs
———————————————
Total Hours Worked

Offers Made
———————————————
Offers Accepted

Employees Terminating
———————————————
Total Employees

Satisfied Employees
———————————————
Total Employees

Information Systems

Output Distributed
on Time
———————————————
Total Output Distributed

Hardware Uptime
———————————————
Total Hardware Time

Out of Service Terminals
———————————————
Total # Terminals

Trouble Calls Received
———————————————
*Unit of Time (Week,
Month, Etc.)*

Keypunch Earned Hours
———————————————
Keypunch Actual Hours

Jobs Completed
———————————————
Jobs Scheduled

Sales/Value Added Sales
———————————————
*Information Systems
Head Count*

Total Operations Head
Count
———————————————
*Information Systems
Head Count*

Operations Budget
———————————————
*Information Systems
Budget*

User Complaints
———————————————
Hours of Usage

Proj. Estimated
Development Cost
———————————————
*Proj. Actual
Development Cost*

Information Systems Cost
———————————————
Revenue

Terminals
———————————————
 # Employees

EXAMPLES OF MICROMEASUREMENTS BY FUNCTION (continued)

Product Assurance

$$\frac{\text{PA Dept. Hours}}{\textit{Production Hours}}$$

$$\frac{\text{PA Indirect Hours}}{\textit{Total Quality Hours}}$$

$$\frac{\text{Earned Hours}}{\textit{Direct Hours}}$$

$$\frac{\text{Cost of Quality}}{\textit{Cost of Sales}}$$

$$\frac{\text{Sales/Value Added Sales}}{\textit{Product Assurance Head Count}}$$

$$\frac{\text{Total Receiving Insp. Hours}}{\textit{Lots Received}}$$

$$\frac{\text{Material Lots Inspected}}{\textit{Receiving Inspection Head Count}}$$

$$\frac{\text{Total Operating Head Count}}{\textit{PA Dept. Head Count}}$$

$$\frac{\text{Operations Budget}}{\textit{PA Dept. Budget}}$$

$$\frac{\text{Production Earned Hours}}{\textit{Quality Eng. Support Hours}}$$

$$\frac{\text{Quality Engineering Support Costs}}{\textit{Production Labor Burden Material Costs}}$$

$$\frac{\text{Errors on Inspection Procedures}}{\textit{Inspection Procedures Issued}}$$

$$\frac{\text{Errors in Data Collection}}{\textit{Volume of Data Collected}}$$

$$\frac{\text{Actual Burden Rate}}{\textit{Planned Burden Rate}}$$

$$\frac{\text{Prevention Costs}}{\textit{Cost of Quality}}$$

$$\frac{\text{Appraisal Costs}}{\textit{Cost of Quality}}$$

$$\frac{\text{Failure Costs}}{\textit{Cost of Quality}}$$

$$\frac{\text{\# Quality Engineering on Engineering Progs.}}{\textit{Total \# Quality Engineering}}$$

Material

$$\frac{\text{Purchase Order Errors}}{\textit{Purchase Orders Audited}}$$

$$\frac{\text{Estimated Savings on Orders Placed}}{\textit{Dollar Value of Orders Placed}}$$

$$\frac{\text{Material Proposal Records Received}}{\textit{Material Proposal Records Completed}}$$

$$\frac{\text{Incoming Material Lots Accepted}}{\textit{Incoming Material Lots}}$$

$$\frac{\text{\$ Amount of Purchases}}{\textit{Purchasing Dept. Head Count}}$$

$$\frac{\text{Procurement Dept. Budget}}{\textit{Purchase Orders Issued}}$$

$$\frac{\text{\# POs Placed}}{\textit{Purchasing Dept. Head Count}}$$

$$\frac{\text{Total Operations Head Count}}{\textit{Purchasing Dept. Head Count}}$$

$$\frac{\text{Sales/Value Added Sales}}{\textit{Procurement Dept. Head Count}}$$

$$\frac{\text{\$ Amount of Purchases}}{\textit{Purchasing Dept. Budget}}$$

$$\frac{\text{Vendor Lots on Time}}{\textit{Vendor Lots Received}}$$

EXAMPLES OF MICROMEASUREMENTS BY FUNCTION (continued)

Communications

$$\frac{\text{Reproduction Costs}}{\textit{\# Pages Produced}}$$

$$\frac{\text{Viewgraphs Redone}}{\textit{Total Viewgraphs Produced}}$$

$$\frac{\text{Sales/Value Added Sales}}{\textit{Communications Dept. Head Count}}$$

$$\frac{\text{Operations Head Count}}{\textit{Communications Dept. Head Count}}$$

$$\frac{\text{Cost of Viewgraph Change}}{\textit{Total Graphics Cost}}$$

Finance

$$\frac{\text{Trade Billed Receivables}}{\textit{Avg. Trade Billed Sales/Day}}$$

$$\frac{\text{Invoices Processed x Standard}}{\textit{Disbursement Audit Hours}}$$

$$\frac{\text{Total Operations Personnel}}{\textit{Finance Personnel}}$$

$$\frac{\text{Net Assets}}{\textit{Sales}}$$

$$\frac{\text{\# Pricing Proposals}}{\textit{\# Pricing People}}$$

$$\frac{\text{Operations Budget}}{\textit{Finance Dept. Budget}}$$

$$\frac{\text{Sales/Value Added Sales}}{\textit{Finance Personnel}}$$

$$\frac{\text{Profit Dollars}}{\textit{Payrool Dollars}}$$

$$\frac{\text{Receivables Over 60 Days}}{\textit{Total Receivables}}$$

$$\frac{\text{Incomplete Cost Standard}}{\textit{Total Cost Standards}}$$

$$\frac{\text{Finance Dept. Budget}}{\textit{Sales}}$$

$$\frac{\text{\$ Value of Pricing Proposal}}{\textit{\# Pricing People}}$$

$$\frac{\text{Invoicing Errors}}{\textit{Invoices Processed}}$$

$$\frac{\text{Customer Satisfaction Index Net Billings}}{\textit{Indirect Head Count}}$$

EXAMPLES OF MICROMEASUREMENTS BY FUNCTION (continued)

General/Miscellaneous

$$\frac{\text{Actual Hrs./\$}}{\textit{Estimated Hrs./\$}}$$

$$\frac{\text{Direct Head Count}}{\textit{Indirect Head Count}}$$

$$\frac{\text{Operations Head Count}}{\textit{Department Head Count}}$$

$$\frac{\text{Operations Sales/Value Added Sales}}{\textit{Department Head Count}}$$

$$\frac{\text{Building Sq. Footage}}{\textit{Maintenance Cleaning Personnel}}$$

$$\frac{\text{Maintenance Orders Within Estimate}}{\textit{Total Maintenance Orders}}$$

$$\frac{\text{Unplanned Absent Hours}}{\textit{Total Hours}}$$

$$\frac{\text{Pages Produced}}{\textit{Word Processing Head Count}}$$

$$\frac{\text{Backlog Hrs. on Maintenance Work Orders}}{\textit{Maintenance Head Count}}$$

$$\frac{\text{Nonproductive Time}}{\textit{Total Time Available}}$$

$$\frac{\text{Department Costs}}{\textit{Department Budgeted Costs}}$$

$$\frac{\text{Head Count}}{\textit{\# Secretaries}}$$

$$\frac{\text{\# People in QC Teams}}{\textit{Total Employees}}$$

$$\frac{\text{Sales}}{\textit{Assets}}$$

$$\frac{\text{Profit}}{\textit{Employees}}$$

$$\frac{\text{Facilities Cost}}{\textit{Facilities Sq. Ft.}}$$

$$\frac{\text{Assets}}{\textit{Employees}}$$

PERFORMANCE IMPROVEMENT PROCESS

Performance improvement is a continuous process. It requires a commitment at all levels—individual, group, department, and division—and in all job functions

The guide establishes seven steps, or sequential actions, you must take to improve performance. Each of them will lead you in the right direction toward achieving quality of work, quality of work life, and quality of management. The diagram on page 218 summarizes the seven action improvement steps.

Action 1. Establish the Management and Cultural Environment— The first step that affects this whole process is establishing the needed environment to effect change. The guidelines show how to involve others in an effective way to bring about performance improvement.

Action 2. Define the Mission—It's important that the action group delineates its reason for existence, its purpose for continuing in business, and a list of its products and services. To be effective it must be doing the right things as well as doing things right.

SEVEN STEPS FOR PERFORMANCE IMPROVEMENT

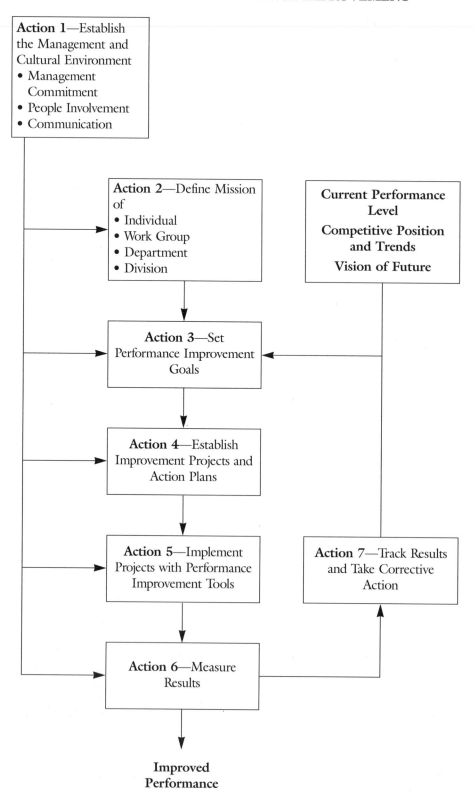

Action 1—Establish the Management and Cultural Environment
• Management Commitment
• People Involvement
• Communication

Action 2—Define Mission of
• Individual
• Work Group
• Department
• Division

Current Performance Level

Competitive Position and Trends

Vision of Future

Action 3—Set Performance Improvement Goals

Action 4—Establish Improvement Projects and Action Plans

Action 5—Implement Projects with Performance Improvement Tools

Action 7—Track Results and Take Corrective Action

Action 6—Measure Results

Improved Performance

Action 3. Set Performance Improvement Goals—Assess your current performance level competitive position, your vision of the future, and your present goals. Then define your overall improvement goals before you choose your specific performance improvement project(s) and the mini-goals associated with it.

Action 4. Establish Improvement Plans—Determine what aspects need improvement, how much you should change, and when it is necessary to change. Look at your group from a perfect world model and a cost driver viewpoint. Then define plans for improvement.

Action 5. Implement Projects Utilizing Performance Improvement Tools—Employ the fundamental elements of good management in promoting performance improvements. And make use of the many tools available to ensure that you improve performance successfully.

Action 6. Measure Results—Develop ongoing measurements that keep track of your progress against your mini-goals as well as your ultimate goal. Be sure that these measurements are easy to understand and that they effectively provide an indication of success or failure.

Action 7. Track Results and Take Corrective Action—To determine your planned progress against plan, compare your results with your goals. Take corrective actions whenever your goals are not being met.

DEFINITIONS AND RESOURCES

This glossary summarizes the terms, acronyms, and processes used in the book. It provides some sources for help—both books and consultants, but does not include *all* the terms, books, or consultants. It reflects books I have found useful, and consultants from which I have learned or with which I am familiar.

American Society for Quality Control (ASQC)

ASQC is the primary organization in the United States for promoting quality practices and total quality management. ASQC, 611 E. Wisconsin Ave., Milwaukee, WI 53202; 800-248-1946.

Association for Quality and Participation (AQP)

AQP started as the International Association for Quality Circles. The organization has broadened its goals toward total quality. AQP, 801 B W. 8th St., Cincinnati, OH 45203; 513-381-1959.

Cause-and-Effect Diagram

Sometimes called an Ishikawa diagram or a fishbone diagram; it was first used by Ishikawa in Japan in the 1940s. It provides pictorial relationships between the many possible causes of a given effect.

Using the diagram involves group brainstorming to create a list of causes and group involvement to organize the causes under the appropriate headings.

It is a powerful tool to bring the group to a consensus of causes and to support their establishing a meaningful priority to pursue solution of the effect.

The process is described in *Guide to Quality Control* by Kaoru Ishikawa (Tokyo: Asian Productivity Organization, 1976).

Cause-and-Effect Diagram with Cards (CEDAC)

CEDAC is an adaptation of the original Ishikawa diagram for promoting a higher level of involvement and ownership.

This process first develops a basic cause-and-effect diagram. The key difference is that users have the freedom to add information on a continuous basis. The result is a living diagram that is continuously changing, not waiting for an update at a monthly or weekly meeting.

Managerial Engineering by Ryuji Fukuda (Cambridge, Mass.: Productivity Press, 1983) provides details on the application of this process plus other key management techniques, such as stockless production (JIT).

Cost of Quality (COQ)

COQ is a measure of how the time of each person in an organization is spent. The process separates work into that which is meaningful, work spent in preventing errors, and work spent correcting errors. Data can be expanded to include materials and facilities. COQ allows an organization access to data proving the need for a focus on quality.

An excellent resource for this process is Philip B. Crosby's book *Quality Is Free* (New York: McGraw-Hill and ASQC Quality Press, 1979).

Design of Experiments

This is a process for optimizing a design or set of manufacturing variables using the least number of experiments.

This technique, also called fractional factorial statistics, allows a process with many variables to be analyzed for the optimum combination in one-third or less of the tests otherwise needed. The benefits are cost savings on experimental runs and the optimization of the process with high accuracy as compared to traditional guesswork techniques, or 100-percent testing of all variable combinations.

A number of excellent texts are available from ASQC Quality Press. For a free catalog of publications, call 800-248-1946.

Employee Involvement Association
See Suggestion System

Job Content Analysis
In this process a statistical technique is used to sample what a person does and to provide data on how time is really spent. These data then allow analysis of the tasks to determine if they are being done by the right person or even in the right department.

The Extensor System of professional- and management-level work measurement was invented in Sweden and developed in the United States. Its extensive use by organizations and individuals has helped optimize job cost definitions using the least amount of time and work interruptions. The system is applicable to a wide variety of job types where the employee makes decisions regarding how the job sequence and content are managed. For training and consulting contact Dr. John Robertsen of The Extensor Corporation, 17273 Hampton Ct., Minnetonka, MN 55345; 612-935-0627.

Just-in-Time (JIT)
JIT is a process leading to stockless production where needed materials arrive at an operation just in time. The benefits of a JIT system are significant.

1. Reduced work in process (WIP)
2. Reduced salvage or scrap when a fault is identified (few parts to scrap)
3. Quick identification of faulty product when it doesn't work at the next operation (minutes later)
4. Higher product quality; fewer products are included in parts not meeting requirements
5. Reduced inventory costs
6. Shorter lead time to make changes

See Richard J. Schonberger's book, *Japanese Manufacturing Techniques* (New York: The Free Press, 1982), and *Kanban: Just in* 223

Time at Toyota by the Japan Management Association (Cambridge, Mass.: Productivity Press, 1986).

Kanban

This is a process most often attributed to the Toyota developments where materials are replaced as they are used. Cards or similar devices to indicate needs. Kanban is integral to most just-in-time actions.

Malcolm Baldrige National Quality Award

Public Law 100–107 established an annual quality award for the United States. The award has become a measure of business excellence in the years since its adoption. See Chapter 4 for details. Contact ASQC for more information.

Profit Sharing/Gain Sharing

These two terms that are frequently used interchangeably. They are, however, different.

Profit sharing is a process that shares with employees some specified amount or percentage of profits. It provides a sense of ownership through the sharing process. It lacks a feeling of control since the profit is a function of both employee efficiency and market price. Since price cannot be controlled, profit sharing is not predictable.

Gain sharing is a process that measures gains in productivity caused by employee-identified changes in labor or material used. The gain-sharing concept can be applied to small work groups and can reinforce team or circle reviews of the process. It is applicable to office, service, or manufacturing operations. It is easy to establish ownership and measure the impact of what a group of employees accomplished. It shares a percent of the dollars saved either to each small work group or as an average to the whole company. Gain sharing is an excellent process with circles, and it reinforces use of statistics or other techniques of problem solving. It ties directly to a suggestion system.

Scanlon plans is another term used for employee participation in the outcome of the business. Joseph N. Scanlon was a cost accountant that became a union leader. He developed his approach after the closing of the steel company where he was employed. The Scanlon plan shares savings in employee labor. It also includes a suggestion process. Scanlon died in 1956.

There are numerous books on profit sharing, gain sharing, and Scanlon plans. Another resource is the Profit Sharing Council of America, 20 N. Wacker Drive, Suite 1722, Chicago, IL 60606; 312-372-3416.

Quality of Work Life (QWL)

The recognition of job satisfaction as a basis for employee productivity is summarized in the concept of quality of work life. This concept relates the needs of all employees for dignity, a feeling of self-worth, and ownership, in addition to a clean, safe workplace and assurance of continued employment.

A field of study and application for QWL has emerged as sociotechnical systems where the needs of the person and those of technology can be effectively brought together.

Eric Trist is considered the first QWL researcher based on his studies in Europe after World War I. He has extensive publications along with numerous other authors.

A source for material is: American Center for Quality of Worklife, 37 Tip Top Way, Berkeley Heights, NJ 07922; 908-464-8080.

Quality Function Deployment (QFD)

QFD is a process for translating customer requirements into the appropriate company specifications. The process graphically compares customer requirements, product features, and competitive products and ranks each of the relationships. The resulting diagram is frequently called the *house of quality* because of its shape. QFD requires the use of decision-making tools to resolve many of the identified problems.

Quality Press

A division of the American Society for Quality Control (ASQC) and the largest publisher of quality-related books.

Seven Basic Tools

These seven tools are the easiest to use and form the backbone of any quality program. All of them are effective in graphically representing data. This representation is vital to communication between members of the quality team, management, and others. *The seven tools are: cause-and-effect diagram, control chart, flowchart, histogram, Pareto chart, run or trend chart, and scatter diagram.*

Some of these tools are described in detail in the team problem-solving section of the appendixes.

Seven New Management Tools

Recent publications from Japan have identified seven new tools for problem solving. Some of these are simple to use and others are very complex. The seven tools and a brief description are as follows:

225

Affinity diagram—This process collects data or opinions about a broad concern and groups the data into clusters. Each item in a cluster has an affinity for the other items. This allows visual and functional grouping of data. (An option for use instead of NGT.)

Arrow diagram—This is not a new process since it is essentially the PERT (Program Evaluation and Review Technique) process of the 1950s. The chart graphs the optional paths of a process showing lead times or other factors in recognizable form.

Interrelationship diagram—This presentation takes the data from an affinity diagram and portrays relationships between the clusters, thus showing major cause-and-effect connections.

Matrix diagram—This uses a diagram much like the systematic diagram but adds specific work assignments for problem solution. It links organizational units with problems and corrective action assignments.

Matrix data analysis (Glyph)—This is a statistical technique to identify the strengths of the relationships between product and process characteristics.

Program decision process chart—These charts help determine which process to use by analyzing the sequence of events and the probable outcomes.

Systematic diagram—This is also known as a tree diagram where relationships between problems and actions are portrayed. The chart looks much like a traditional organization chart.

Shewhart Cycle
The Plan-Do-Check-Act or PDCA circle is used to show the relationship of the steps in finding a solution and the need to continuously repeat the steps for improvement. (See figure on page 149.)

Single Minute Exchange of Dies (SMED)
This concept of tooling design allows rapid changeover from one piece part to another, thus permitting very small economical runs.

SMED identifies concepts that standardize variations in die size and its location such that change can be made without adjustments to the machine and with a minimum of work or special fixtures.

This concept is applicable to all types of machinery (lathes, punch press, plastic mold, and so on).

The SMED concept is fundamental to accomplishing JIT or stockless production. Rapid tooling change supports economic production of small lots and helps reduce scrap and salvage costs. See *A Revolution in Manufacturing—The SMED System,* by Shigeo Shingo (Cambridge, Mass.: Productivity Press, 1985).

Statistical Process Control (SPC) and
Statistical Quality Control (SQC)

SPC and SQC are statistical methods to track process variance (changes) or to predict the capability of a process to meet specifications.

SPC uses a wide range of statistical techniques ranging from simple to complex. Most organizations will be able to effect improvements using the simple techniques.

Statistics allow data to be presented visually or graphically allowing easy understanding of how well a given process is working

The process is applicable to identify product quality in either the office or factory.

A parallel process, SQC, uses the same methods and is usually seen as identical. Some think that SQC concentrates on measurement of product variance while SPC tries to prevent product variance.

Extensive resources exist. Your local ASQC chapter will have both experience and constants. ASQC Quality Press publishes a variety of books, many with a focus on specific kinds of businesses.

Suggestion System

This is a structured process to encourage employees or customers to submit ideas for improvement.

The system can either solicit problems or problems and a suggested solution. Some systems allow either method to be used.

Systems formalize the process and require a written response to each idea. Savings can be calculated and cash or other awards granted based on savings.

Suggestion systems are effective as a separate program or operated in conjunction with quality circles and task teams.

Details are available from the Employee Involvement Association at 703-524-3424; 1735 N. Lynn St. #950, Arlington, VA 22209; and Total Quality Systems, 465 W. Eagle Lake Dr., Maple Grove, MN 55369; 612-424-2260.

William Tracey's book, *Human Resources Management and Development Handbook* (New York: Amacom, 1985) contains details on suggestion systems and other processes.

Total Quality Control (TQC) and
Total Quality Management (TQM)

TQC is a concept that involves all employees in creating quality product. Product is defined as what you produce and pass to another person. This means lathe operators, assemblers, secretaries, managers, engineers, and others, all monitor the quality of what they produce and attempt to achieve zero defects in parts, memos, designs, and the like.

This process is based on everyone having responsibility for the quality of their work. Current traditional processes use a quality control function to find errors (detection) and help identify methods for prevention.

The concept appears simple but TQC really reflects a major change in the attitudes, responsibilities, and ownership of all employees. The concept will cause changes in responsibility and job content. The result is a large reduction in errors made and resulting cost savings in labor and material. The following books are good sources of information: *Japanese Manufacturing Techniques* by Richard J. Schonberger (New York: The Free Press, 1982); and *What Is Total Quality Control* by Kaoru Ishikawa, translated by David J. Lu (Englewood Cliffs, N.J.: Prentice-Hall, 1985).

Value Engineering/Value Analysis (VE/VA)

Originally used in the review of product designs either before production release or even after several years of manufacture. VE/VA is a structured analytical process that supports analysis of all elements of a product leading to improvements in quality, cost, and operation.

The process renamed value analysis to support the broadened use of the methods. Significant improvements using VA have been made in merchandising, office, hospital, and other service industries.

The process was initiated in the United States many years ago. The largest users are in Japan, where it is recognized as a powerful tool. Training is available from Professional Value Services, 2000 Aldrich Ave., South, Minneapolis, MN 55405; 612-870-8509; and the Society of American Value Engineers (SAVE), 60 Revere Drive, Suite 500, Westbrook, IL 60062; 708-480-1730.

Work Simplification/Work Flow Analysis (WS/WFA)

This is a logical method for collecting data about a process and charting it so that a team can effectively consider options for the best solution.

The process of work simplification was effectively used during World War II. It is a key analysis tool used with teams or by individuals since the 1950s.

The process is widely used around the world and is frequently included in the teaching of statistical process control. The two skills reinforce each other and result in a far greater competency for problem solving.

228

Work simplification is accredited to Allan Mogensen who taught it and continually improved it during his lifetime. One of his pupils and friends, Dr. Ben Graham, Jr., has further improved the process and is a principal resource for training and supporting software. His address and phone number are 6600 Troy-Frederic Rd., Tipp City, OH 45371; 513-667-3380.

Zero Defects (ZD)

This concept originated in the 1950s to encourage quality as part of the military procurement process.

Zero defects is based on the fact that the costs of making errors or correcting faulty parts far exceed the costs to do it right the first time. Also, we cannot afford the costs of scrap and salvage and be competitive in world markets.

Philip B. Crosby is the recognized leader in this philosophy and has trained thousands of managers in the concept at his Quality College in Winter Park, Florida. He wrote *Quality Is Free* (New York: McGraw-Hill and ASQC Quality Press, 1979).

The process involves a measurement of the cost of nonquality or the costs associated with making and correcting errors. This cost process then stimulates problem solving and error prevention. The process is applicable to service organizations as well as to manufacturing.

BIBLIOGRAPHY

Abegglen. James C., and George Stalk Jr. *Kaisha: The Japanese Corporation*. New York: Basic Books, 1985.

Christopher, Robert C. *The Japanese Mind: The Goliath Explained*. New York: Simon and Schuster (Linden Books), 1983.

Covey, Stephen R. *The Seven Habits of Highly Effective People*. New York: Simon and Schuster, 1989.

Crosby, Philip B. *Quality Is Free*. New York: McGraw-Hill and ASQC Quality Press, 1979.

Deming, W. Edwards. *Quality, Productivity, and the Competitive Edge*. Cambridge, Mass.: Massachusetts Institute of Technology Press, 1982.

Fukuda, Ryuji. *Managerial Engineering*. Cambridge, Mass.: Productivity Press, 1983.

Hatakeyama, Yoshio. *Manager Revolution*. Cambridge, Mass.: Productivity Press, 1985.

Imai, Masaaki. *Kaizen: The Key to Competitive Success*. New York: Random House, 1986.

Ishikawa, Kaoru. *Guide to Quality Control*. Tokyo: Asian Productivity Organization, 1976.

Japan Management Association. *Kanban: Just in Time at Toyota*. Cambridge, Mass.: Productivity Press, 1986.

Lincoln, James A. *Incentive Management*. Cleveland, Oh.: Lincoln Electric Company, 1951.

Miller, Lawrence M. *American Spirit: Visions of a New Corporate Culture*. New York: William Morrow and Co., 1984.

Mizuno, Shigeru. *The Seven New QC Tools: Management for Quality Improvement.* Cambridge, Mass.: Productivity Press, 1988.

Montgomery, Douglas C. *Design and Analysis of Experiments.* New York: John Wiley & Sons, 1984.

Persico, John Jr. *The TQM Transformation: A Model for Change.* White Plains, N.Y.: Quality Resources, 1992.

Peters, Thomas J., and Robert H. Waterman, Jr. *In Search of Excellence.* New York: Warner Books, 1982.

Schonberger, Richard J. *Japanese Manufacturing Techniques.* New York: The Free Press, 1982.

Shingo, Shigeo. *A Revolution in Manufacturing: The SMED System.* Cambridge, Mass.: Productivity Press, 1985.

————. *Study of Toyota Production System.* Cambridge, Mass.: Productivity Press, 1984.

————. *A Study of the Toyota Production System.* Revised translation. Cambridge, Mass.: Productivity Press, 1989.

————. *Zero Quality Control: Source Inspection and the Poka-Yoke System.* Cambridge, Mass.: Productivity Press, 1986.

Sproul, R. C. *Stronger Than Steel: The Wayne Alderson Story.* San Francisco: Harper & Row, 1980.

Vogel, Ezra F. *Japan as Number One: Lessons for America.* Cambridge, Mass.: Harvard University Press, 1979.